T0355741

The Phenomenology of Internal Time-Consciousness

EDMUND HUSSERL

The Phenomenology of
Internal Time-Consciousness

EDITED BY MARTIN HEIDEGGER

TRANSLATED BY JAMES S. CHURCHILL

INTRODUCTION BY CALVIN O. SCHRAG

INDIANA UNIVERSITY PRESS

This book is a publication of

Indiana University Press
Office of Scholarly Publishing
Herman B Wells Library 350
1320 East 10th Street
Bloomington, Indiana 47405 USA

iupress.indiana.edu

Second printing 2019
© 1964 by Indiana University Press
All rights reserved

Manufactured in the United States of America

Cataloging information is available from the Library of Congress.

Originally cataloged as LCCN 64010829; ISBN 0-253-200970

ISBN 978-0-253-04196-8 (paperback)
ISBN 978-0-253-04199-9 (web PDF)

2 3 4 5 6   24 23 22 21 20 19

CONTENTS

Part Two

Addenda and Supplements to the Analysis of
Time-Consciousness from the Years 1905–1910

INTRODUCTION

The present volume is a translation of Edmund Husserl's *Vorlesungen zur Phänomenologie des inneren Zeitbewusstseins*. With this translation Professor Churchill has rendered to the English-speaking world a service of inestimable value. In the light of the resurgence of interest in the philosophy of Husserl and the development of phenomenology more generally a translation of Husserl's important but often neglected lectures on the phenomenology of the internal time-consciousness is long overdue, and we owe Professor Churchill a great deal for making accessible to the English reader this particular aspect of Husserl's philosophical contribution. A translation is never an easy undertaking, and the value of the services performed by the translator are often overlooked. A good translation requires both a technical knowledge of the language and a fundamental grasp of the subject matter. The present translation is commendable on both counts. It remains grammatically true to the original text and succeeds in capturing the spirit of Husserl's philosophy.

Phenomenology, since the foundations of its program were laid by Husserl, has always received serious attention on the Continent. In the United States and Great Britain, however, its impact has been somewhat delayed. Although it has been the subject of discussion for some time in various isolated philosophical circles in the English-speaking world, not until recently has it made its way into the mainstream of contemporary Anglo-American thought. This is in some respects puzzling, for the phenomenological approach is not alien to

American philosophical soil. William James, for whom Husserl always had a great admiration, not only dealt with phenomenological issues but did so in a way that exhibits striking parallels to the method of Husserl. James' interest in the structure of human consciousness and his suggestions regarding the intentional nature of knowledge afford a link between American pragmatism and German phenomenology which merits further exploration. Currently there is some interest in investigating the parallels between phenomenology and Anglo-American linguistic philosophy. Although it is well to caution against a too easy *rapprochement* between these two traditions, it would appear that the meanings disclosed in the usages of ordinary language are significantly akin to those explicated by the language of the *"Lebenswelt."* It would thus be a fair inference that the task of philosophy is envisioned by these two traditions in a not wholly dissimilar way.

One of the more distinctive characteristics of the phenomenological movement is its cultural pervasiveness. Its impact has been discernible in studies on perception, psychology, psychiatry, ethics, religion, art, and education. Husserl himself was quite aware of the relevance of his investigations to the various areas in the cultural and historical life of man. Although the primary task which he assumed was that of laying the foundations (which in a sense have to be laid anew for each generation), his writings offer fertile suggestions for phenomenological investigations in the special areas of the humanities and the social sciences. He did not have the time to carry through these investigations, but he did provide the impulse and the methodological tools for his phenomenological successors. The continuation of this impulse and the refined elaboration of these tools is discernible in such provocative works as Merleau-Ponty's *Phenomenology of Perception,* Nicolai Hartmann's *Ethics,* Max Scheler's *The Nature of Sympathy,* Rudolph Otto's *The Idea of the Holy,* Paul Tillich's *The Courage to Be,* and Alfred Schutz's *The Problems of*

Social Reality—not to mention the direct influence of Husserl's thought on Martin Heidegger's *Being and Time* and Jean-Paul Sartre's *Being and Nothingness*.

In the thought of Husserl, as in the thought of every great philosopher, one can trace stages of development. He deepened his investigations and matured his reflections as he moved from the University of Halle (1887–1901) to Göttingen (1901–1916) and then to Freiburg (1916–1929). It was during his career at Freiburg, as well as during the period following his retirement, that he assimilated his later and mature reflections with his earlier insights. It was this whole course of development that gave to the world the seminal ideas of phenomenological philosophy. Some of the main themes and ideas that emerged throughout this development were: a critique of psychologism, the intentionality of consciousness, the phenomenological and eidetic reduction, the phenomenological ego, transcendental intersubjectivity, time-consciousness, and the life-world. Husserl's approach to these phenomenological issues, however, was never that of the system-builder. He abhorred system-building as much as did Kierkegaard and Nietzsche. He was always a beginner, reexamining the foundations of his investigations, resisting all fixed formulations and final conclusions. Philosophy for Husserl was a never-ending pursuit of serious and open-ended questions, which lead to further questions that may require a resetting of the original questions. This at the same time accounts for the fertility of his investigations and for the philosophical freedom which his whole philosophy illustrates.

What place does Husserl's essay on the internal time-consciousness have in his over-all historical and ideational development? The first part of the essay was originally presented as the content of a lecture course at the University of Göttingen in the winter semester of 1904–1905. The second part is based on additional and supplementary lectures which he gave on the subject between 1905 and 1910. The period which spanned the formulation and development of the ideas contained in the present work constituted an interim between the publication of the second volume of his *Logical Investigations* (1901) and his *Ideas: General Introduction to Pure Phenomenology* (1913). Although Husserl published very little during these intervening years, this interim was a kind of ripening period for his philosophical ideas, as is evidenced by his lectures on time. The significance of these lectures did not become immediately apparent, either because of an apathetic philosophical audience or because of historical factors in the development of philosophy in Germany at the time. It was not until 1928 that the lectures were compiled and published by Husserl's former student, Martin Heidegger.

The significance of the content of these compiled lectures can hardly be overemphasized. During his University of Halle period Husserl was interested in formulating a philosophical logic which would undercut any and all psychological reductivisms. In his Göttingen lectures the attention shifts from an interest in logic to an interest in the structure of consciousness. It is in these lectures that Husserl first makes explicit his doctrine of intentionality, which he took over from his former teacher, Franz Brentano, and then redefined so as to free it from all vestiges of psychologism. All forms of perception, according to Husserl, presuppose an intentional structure of consciousness, and it is in this intentional structure that the primordial link between consciousness and the world is to be sought. This theme of intentionality is then developed and more fully elaborated in his *Ideas,* which appeared three years after the completion of his lectures comprised in the present volume. Also, in the present volume one finds penetrating studies on phantasy, imagination, memory, and recollection. The distinctive contribution of these lectures, however, is Husserl's exploration of the terrain of consciousness in the light of its temporality. Hence the significance and appropriateness of the title: *The Phenomenology of Internal Time-Consciousness.* Consciousness is qualified by temporal determinants. Temporality provides the form for perception, phantasy, imagination, memory, and recollection. In these lectures the two "categories" of temporality, retention and protention, which play such an important role in his subsequent thought, are stated and clarified. The distinction between cosmic and phenomenological time, which was so decisive in the development of existentialism, is delineated; and the relevance of phenomenological time for the constitution of temporal objects is discussed. All these themes were later developed more extensively in his *Ideas* and continued to hold his interest until the end of his philosophical career, as is evidenced by his *Nachlass* (presently housed in the Husserl Archives at the University of Louvain). The unpublished manuscripts have been collected and grouped under various headings, providing a kind of classification of his later philosophical interests. Of particular relevance for the present essay are the collected manuscripts entitled *Zeitkonstitution als formale Konstitution* (designated in the archives as "Manuskripten C"). A study of these manuscripts will show that his early Göttingen lectures not only provide the tone for his subsequent philosophical investigations but also state the basic problems with which Husserl was concerned until the very end. To be sure, significant reformulations take place throughout his philosophical maturation, but a discernible continuity is apparent as one moves from the early to the later Husserl.

Both the Husserl scholar and the general philosophical reader will benefit from this translation. It will provide the scholar with material for further examination of the significance of time in the thought of Husserl. It will provide the general reader with some of the methodological procedures and governing concepts in a type of philosophy which is eliciting increasing interest in various philosophical circles in the English-speaking world.

CALVIN O. SCHRAG

Purdue University

13

EDITOR'S FOREWORD

The following analysis of the "phenomenology of internal time-consciousness" falls into two sections. The first includes the last part of a four-hour lecture course held during the winter semester in Göttingen, 1904–1905. The course was entitled: "Important Points Concerning Phenomenology and Theory of Knowledge." While the second volume of *Logische Untersuchungen* (1901) had as a theme the interpretation of the "higher" act of cognition, these lectures were to investigate "the most deeply underlying intellective acts: perception, phantasy [*Phantasie*], figurative consciousness, memory, and the intuition of time." The second section is derived from supplements to the course and from later studies (to 1910).

Continuing studies of time-consciousness in connection with the problem of individuation, especially those undertaken since 1917, are reserved for a later publication.

The pervading theme of the present study is the temporal constitution of a pure datum of sensation and the self-constitution of "phenomenological time" which underlies such a constitution. The exposition of the intentional character of time-consciousness and the developing fundamental elucidation of *intentionality* in general is basic to this study. This alone, apart from the particular content of individual analyses, makes the following study an indispensable supplement to the basic clarification of intentionality first taken up in *Logische Untersuchungen*. Even today, this term "intentionality" is no all-explanatory word but one which designates a central *problem*.

It is apparent that, apart from refinements not affecting the style, the text retains the lively character of the lectures themselves. The repetitions of important analyses, always varying to be sure, are deliberately retained in the interest of a concrete check of the understanding of the reader.

In some instances, the chapter and paragraph divisions were inserted in the stenographic transcription by Frl. Dr. Stein to conform in part to the marginal notes of the author.

MARTIN HEIDEGGER

Marburg a.d.L., April 1928

The Phenomenology of Internal Time-Consciousness

THE LECTURES ON INTERNAL TIME-CONSCIOUSNESS FROM THE YEAR 1905

THE LECTURES ON INTERNAL TIME-CONSCIOUSNESS FROM THE YEAR 1905

Introduction

The analysis of time-consciousness is an age-old crux of descriptive psychology and theory of knowledge. The first thinker to be deeply sensitive to the immense difficulties to be found here was Augustine, who labored almost to despair over this problem. Chapters 13–18 of Book XI of the *Confessions* must even today be thoroughly studied by everyone concerned with the problem of time. For no one in this knowledge-proud modern generation has made more masterful or significant progress in these matters than this great thinker who struggled so earnestly with the problem. One may still say with Augustine: *si nemo a me quaerat, scio, si quaerenti explicare velim, nescio.*

Naturally, we all know what time is; it is that which is most familiar. However, as soon as we make the attempt to account for time-consciousness, to put Objective [1] time and

1. [Following the practice of Dorion Cairns, the translator of Husserl's *Cartesianische Meditationen* (Martinus Nijhoff, The Hague, 1960), to differentiate the terms *Objekt* and *Gegenstand*, both of which are used by Husserl, I have chosen to translate the word *Objekt*

subjective time-consciousness into the right relation and thus gain an understanding of how temporal Objectivity—therefore, individual Objectivity in general—can be constituted in subjective time-consciousness—indeed, as soon as we even make the attempt to undertake an analysis of pure subjective time-consciousness—the phenomenological content of lived experiences of time [*Zeiterlebnisse*]—we are involved in the most extraordinary difficulties, contradictions, and entanglements.

An exposition of Brentano's analysis of time, which, unfortunately, he never published, but imparted only through lectures, can serve as a point of departure for our study. This analysis was presented very briefly by Marty in his paper on the development of the sense of color which appeared in the late seventies. Stumpf also made a brief reference in his *Tonpsychologie*.

§ 1. The Exclusion [Ausschaltung] of Objective [Objektiven] Time

A few general observations must still be made beforehand. Our aim is a phenomenological analysis of time-consciousness. Involved in this, as in any other such analysis, is the complete exclusion of every assumption, stipulation, or conviction concerning Objective time (of all transcendent presuppositions concerning existents). From an Objective point of view every lived experience, like every real being [*Sein*] and moment of being, may have its place in the one unique Objective time—consequently, also the lived experience of the perception and representation [*Vorstellung*] of time itself. It may be of interest to some to determine the Objective time of a lived experience by that of one which is time-constituting.

by *Object* and *Gegenstand* by *object*. The same applies, *mutatis mutandis*, in the case of words derived from *Objekt* and *Gegenstand*. If the English word *object* or any word derived from it stands first in a sentence, the German word is given in brackets. J.S.C.]

22

It may further be an interesting study to establish how time which is posited in a time-consciousness as Objective is related to real Objective time, whether the evaluations of temporal intervals conform to Objective, real temporal intervals or how they deviate from them. But these are not tasks for phenomenology. Just as a real thing or the real world is not a phenomenological datum, so also world-time, real time, the time of nature in the sense of natural science including psychology as the natural science of the psychical, is not such a datum.

When we speak of the analysis of time-consciousness, of the temporal character of objects of perception, memory, and expectation, it may seem, to be sure, as if we assume the Objective flow of time, and then really study only the subjective conditions of the possibility of an intuition of time and a true knowledge of time. What we accept, however, is not the existence of a world-time, the existence of a concrete duration, and the like, but time and duration appearing as such. These, however, are absolute data which it would be senseless to call into question. To be sure, we also assume an existing time; this, however, is not the time of the world of experience but the *immanent time* of the flow of consciousness. The evidence that consciousness of a tonal process, a melody, exhibits a succession even as I hear it is such as to make every doubt or denial appear senseless.

What is meant by the exclusion of Objective time will perhaps become still clearer if we draw a parallel with space, since space and time exhibit so many noted and significant analogies. Consciousness of space belongs in the sphere of phenomenological givens, i.e., the consciousness of space is the lived experience in which "intuition of space" as perception and phantasy takes place. When we open our eyes, we see into Objective space—this means (as reflective observation reveals) that we have a visual content of sensation which establishes an intuition of space, an appearance of things situated in such and such a way. If we abstract all transcendental interpretation and reduce perceptual appearance to the primary given content, the latter yields the continuum of the field of vision, which is something quasi-spatial but not, as it were, space or a plane surface in space. Roughly described, this continuum is a twofold, continuous multiplicity. We discover relations such as juxtaposition, superimposition, interpenetration, unbroken lines which fully enclose a portion of the field, and so on. But these are not Objective-spatial relations. It makes no sense at all, for example, to say that a point of the visual field is one meter away from the corner of this table here or is beside or above it, etc. It makes just as little sense, naturally, to assert that the appearance of a thing has a position in space and various other spatial relations. The appearance of a house is not beside or over the house, one meter from it, etc.

We can now draw similar conclusions with regard to time. The phenomenological data are the apprehensions of time, the lived experiences in which the temporal in the Objective sense appears. Again, phenomenologically given are the moments of lived experience which specifically establish apprehensions of time as such, and, therefore, establish, if the occasion should arise, the specific temporal content (that which conventional nativism calls the primordially temporal). But nothing of this is Objective time. One cannot discover the least trace of Objective time through phenomenological analysis. The "primordial temporal field" is by no means a part of Objective time; the lived and experienced [erlebte] now, taken in itself, is not a point of Objective time, and so on. Objective [Objektiver] space, Objective time, and with them the Objective world of real things and events—these are all transcendencies [Transzendenzen]. In truth, space and reality are not transcendent in a mystical sense. They are not "things in themselves" but just phenomenal space, phenomenal spatio-temporal reality, the appearing spatial form, the appearing temporal form. None of these are lived experiences. And the nexuses of order which are to be found in lived experiences as true immanences are not to be encountered in the empirical Objective order. They do not fit into this order.

A study of the data of place [*Lokaldaten*] (that nativism accepts from a psychological standpoint) which form the immanent order of the "field of visual sensation," and of this field itself, also belongs in a completely worked out phenomenology of space. These data are to appearing regions [*Orten*] as the data of quality are to appearing Objective qualities. If one speaks in the one case of place-signs, he must in the other speak of quality-signs. Sensed red is a phenomenological datum which exhibits an Objective quality animated by a certain function of apprehension. This datum is not itself a quality. Not the sensed but the perceived red is a quality in the true sense, i.e., a characteristic of an appearing thing. Sensed red is red only in an equivocal sense, for red is the name of a real quality. If, with reference to certain phenomenological occurrences, one speaks of a "coincidence" of one with the other, he must still consider that it is through apprehension that sensed red first acquires the value of being a moment which exhibits a material quality. Viewed in itself, however, sensed red is not such a moment. One must also note that the "coincidence" of the exhibitive [*Darstellenden*] and that which is exhibited is by no means the coincidence of a consciousness of identity whose correlate is "one and the same."

If we call a phenomenological datum "sensed" which through apprehension as corporeally given makes us aware of something Objective, which means, then, that it is Objectively perceived, in the same sense we must also distinguish between a "sensed" temporal datum and a perceived temporal datum.[2] The latter signifies Objective time. The former, however, is

2. The term "sensed," therefore, signifies a relational concept which in itself does not tell us whether in general what is sensed is material [*sensuell*], or indeed whether in general it is immanent in the sense of the material. In other words, it remains open whether the sensed is itself already constituted, and perhaps in a way quite other than the material. But this whole distinction is best left aside. Not every constitution has the schema: content of apprehension—apprehension.

25

not itself Objective time (or position in Objective time) but the phenomenological datum through whose empirical apperception the relation to Objective time is constituted. *Temporal data*—or, if you will, temporal signs—are not *tempora* themselves. Objective [*Objektive*] time belongs in the context of empirical objectivity. "Sensed" temporal data are not merely sensed; they are also charged with characters of apprehension, and to these again belong certain requirements and qualifications whose function on the basis of the sensed data is to measure appearing times and time-relations against one another and to bring this or that into an Objective order of one sort or another and seemingly to separate this or that into real orders. Finally, what is constituted here as valid, Objective being [*Sein*] is the one infinite Objective time in which all things and events—material things with their physical properties, minds with their mental states—have their definite temporal positions which can be measured by chronometers.

It may be—and concerning this we need not judge here—that these Objective determinations ultimately have their basis in the substantiation of distinctions and relations of temporal data or in immediate adequation to these temporal data themselves. But a sensed "at the same time" [*Zugleich*], for example, cannot forthwith be equated with Objective simultaneity, the sensed equality of phenomenological-temporal intervals with Objective equality of intervals of time, etc. And the sensed absolute temporal datum cannot forthwith be equated with Objective time as it is experienced. (This also holds for the absolute datum of the now.) Apprehension—specifically, the evident apprehension of a content just as it is experienced —does not yet mean the apprehension of an Objectivity in the empirical sense, i.e., of an Objective reality in the sense of which we speak of Objective things, events, relations, of Objective spatial and temporal situations, of Objectively real spatial and temporal forms, etc.

Let us look at a piece of chalk. We close and open our

eyes. We have two perceptions, but we say of them that we see the same piece of chalk twice. We have, thereby, contents which are separated temporally. We also can see a phenomenological, temporal apartness [*Auseinander*], a separation, but there is no separation in the object. It is the same. In the object there is duration, in the phenomenon, change. Similarly, we can also subjectively sense a temporal sequence where Objectively a coexistence is to be established. The lived and experienced content is "Objectified," and the Object is now constituted from the material of this content in the mode of apprehension. The object, however, is not merely the sum or complexion of this "content," which does not enter into the object at all. The object is more than the content and other than it. Objectivity [*Objektivität*] belongs to "experience," that is, to the unity of experience, to the lawfully experienced context of nature. Phenomenologically speaking, Objectivity is not even constituted through "primary" content but through characters of apprehension and the regularities [*Gesetzmäs-sigkeiten*] which pertain to the essence of these characters. It is precisely the business of the phenomenology of cognition to grasp this fully and to make it completely intelligible.

§ 2. The Question of the "Origin of Time"

In conformity with these reflections, we also understand the difference between the phenomenological question (i.e., from the standpoint of theory of knowledge) and the psychological with regard to the origin of all concepts constitutive of experience, and so also with regard to the question of the origin of time. *From the point of view of theory of knowledge, the question of the possibility of experience* (which, at the same time, is *the question of the essence of experience*) necessitates a return to the phenomenological data of which all that is experienced consists phenomenologically. Since what is experienced is split owing to the antithesis of "authentic" and "unauthentic" ["eigentlich" und "uneigentlich"], and since authentic experience, i.e., the intuitive and ultimately adequate, provides the standard for the evaluation of experience, the phenomenology of "authentic" experience is especially required.

Accordingly, the question of the essence of time leads back to the question of the "origin" of time. The *question of the origin* is oriented toward the *primitive* forms of the consciousness of time in which the primitive differences of the temporal are constituted intuitively and authentically as the originary [*originären*] sources of all certainties relative to time. The question of the origin of time should not be confused with the *question of its psychological origin*—the controversial question between *empiricism and nativism*. With this last question we are asking about the *primordial material of sensation out of which arises Objective intuition of space and time* in the human individual and even in the species. We are indifferent to the question of the empirical genesis. What interest us are lived experiences as regards their objective sense and their descriptive content. Psychological apperception, which views lived experiences as psychical states of empirical persons, i.e., *psycho-physical subjects,* and uncovers relationships, be they purely psychical or psycho-physical, between them, and follows their development, formation, and transformation according to *natural laws*—this psychological apperception is something wholly other than the *phenomenological*. We do not classify lived experiences according to any particular form of reality. We are concerned with reality only insofar as it is intended, represented, intuited, or conceptually thought. With reference to the problem of time, this implies that we are interested in *lived experiences* of time. That these lived experiences themselves are temporally determined in an Objective sense, *that they belong in the world of things and psychical subjects* and have their place therein, their *efficacy,* their empirical origin and their being—that does not concern us, of that we know nothing. On the other hand, it does interest us that "Objective-temporal" data are *intended* in these lived experiences. Acts which belong to the domain of phenomenology can be described as follows: the acts in question intend this or that "Objective" moment; more precisely, these acts are concerned with the exhibition of *a priori* truths which belong to the moments constitutive of Objectivity. We try to clarify the *a priori* of *time* by investigating *time-consciousness,* by bringing its essential constitution to light and, possibly, by setting forth the content of apprehension and act-characters pertaining specifically to time, to which content and characters the *a priori* characters of time are essentially due. Naturally, I am referring here to self-evident laws such as the following: (1) that the fixed temporal order is that of an infinite, two-dimensional series; (2) that two different times can never be conjoint; (3) that their relation is a non-simultaneous one; (4) that there is transitivity, that to every time belongs an earlier and a later; etc.

So much for the general introduction.

S E C T I O N   O N E

BRENTANO'S THEORY CONCERNING THE ORIGIN
OF TIME

§ 3. The Primordial Associations

By coming to grips with Brentano's theory of the origin of time, we shall now gain an approach to the problems we have raised. Brentano believed he had found the solution to the problem in the primordial associations, in the "genesis of the immediate presentations of memory [*Gedächtnisvorstellungen*] which, according to a law that admits no exceptions, are joined to particular presentations of perception without mediation." When we see, hear, or in general perceive something, it happens according to rule that what is perceived remains present for an interval although not without modification. Apart from other alterations, such as those in intensity and richness, which occur now to a lesser, now to a more noticeable degree, there is always yet another and particularly odd characteristic to be confirmed, namely, that anything of this kind remaining in consciousness appears to us as something more or less past, as something temporally shoved back [Zurückgeschobenes], as it were. When, for example, a melody sounds, the individual notes do not completely disappear when the stimulus or the action of the nerve excited by them comes to an end. When the new note sounds, the one just preceding it does not disappear without a trace; otherwise, we should be incapable of observing the relations between the notes which follow one another. We should have a note at every instant, and possibly in the interval between the sounding of the next an empty [leere] phase, but never the idea [Vorstellung] of a melody. On the other hand, it is not merely a matter of presentations of the tones simply persisting in consciousness. Were they to remain unmodified, then instead of a melody we should have a chord of simultaneous notes or rather a disharmonious jumble of sounds such as we should obtain if we struck all the notes simultaneously that have already been sounded. Only in this way, namely, that that peculiar modification occurs, that every aural sensation, after the stimulus which begets it has disappeared, awakes from within itself a similar presentation provided with a temporal determination, and that this determination is continually varied, can we have the presentation of a melody in which the individual notes have their definite place and their definite measure of time.

It is a universal law, therefore, that to each presentation is naturally joined a continuous series of presentations each of which reproduces the content of the preceding but in such a way that the moment of the past is always attached to the new.

Thus, phantasy turns out here in a peculiar way to be productive. We have here the one case in which phantasy in truth creates a new moment of presentation, namely, the temporal moment. Thus, in the sphere of phantasy we have uncovered the origin of ideas of time [*Zeitvorstellungen*]. Psychologists, with the exception of Brentano, have endeavored in vain to discover the true source of these ideas. This failure is due to a blending of subjective and Objective time, always natural to be sure, which confused the psychological researcher and prevented him from seeing the real problem present here. Many are of the opinion that the question of the origin of the concept of time is to be answered in much the same way as the question of the origin of our concepts of colors, sounds, and so on. Thus, just as we sense a color, so also do we sense the duration of the color; just as we sense quality and intensity, so also the temporal duration of an immanent moment of sensation. The external stimulus engenders the quality through the pattern of the physical processes involved, through the kinetic energy of the physical processes, the intensity, and, through the continuation of the stimulus, the subjectively sensed duration. This, however, is an obvious error. To say that the stimulus endures is not to say that the sensation is sensed as enduring but only that the sensation also endures. The duration of sensation and the sensation of duration are different. And it is the same with sensation. The succession of sensations and the sensation of succession are not the same.

We must naturally raise precisely the same objection against those who would trace the idea of duration and succession back to the fact of the duration and succession of the psychical act. Meanwhile, we shall carry out the reflection by applying it specifically to sensation.

Because our ideas do not bear the slightest trace of temporal determinateness, it is conceivable that our sensations could

31

endure or succeed one another without our being aware of it in the least. If we observe, for example, a particular instance of succession and assume that the sensations disappear with the stimuli producing them, we should have a succession of sensations without a notion of a temporal flow. With the emergence of the new sensation we should no longer have any memory of the having-been [*Gewesensein*] of the earlier. In each moment we should have only the consciousness of the sensation just produced and nothing further. But even the continued duration of the sensation already produced would not help us procure the idea of succession. If, in the case of a succession of sounds, the earlier ones were to be preserved as they were while ever new ones were also to sound, we should have a number of sounds simultaneously in our imagination [*Vorstellung*], but not succession. The situation would be no different in the case in which all these sounds sounded at once. Or, to take another example, if, in the case of motion, the body moved were to be held fast unaltered in its momentary position in consciousness, then the space traversed would appear to us to be continuously occupied but we should have no idea of motion. We arrive at the idea of succession only if the earlier sensation does not persist unaltered in consciousness but in the manner described is specifically modified, that is, is continuously modified from moment to moment. In going over into phantasy, the sensation preserves its constantly varying temporal character; from moment to moment the content thus seems to be shoved back more and more. This modification, however, is no longer the business of sensation; it is not brought about through the stimulus. The stimulus produces the actual content of sensation. If the stimulus disappears, the sensation also disappears. But the sensation itself now becomes productive. It produces a phantasy-idea [*Phantasievorstellung*] like, or nearly like, itself with regard to content and enriched by a temporal character. This

32

idea again awakens a new one which is always attached to it, and so on. This continuous joining of a temporally modified idea to those already given Brentano calls "primordial association." As a consequence of this theory, Brentano came to disavow the perception of succession and alteration. We believe that we hear a melody, that we still hear something that is certainly past. However, this is only an illusion which proceeds from the vivacity of primordial association.

§ 4. The Gaining of the Future and Infinite Time

The intuition of time which arises through primordial association is still not intuition of infinite time. It undergoes a further elaboration and, in fact, not only with regard to the past. It obtains an entirely new branch through the addition of the future. On the basis of the appearance of momentary recollections, phantasy forms ideas of the future in a process similar to that through which, circumstances permitting, we arrive at ideas of certain new varieties of color and sound while keeping to known forms and relations. In phantasy, we can transpose a melody which we have heard in a certain key and on the basis of a definite tonal species to different registers. In this way it can very well be that, proceeding from known sounds, we can arrive at sounds which as yet we have never heard. In a similar way—that is to say, in expectation—phantasy forms the idea of the future from the past. The notion that phantasy is able to offer nothing new, that it exhausts itself in the repetition of the same elements already given in perception, is one that is completely erroneous. Finally, what the complete idea of time, the idea of infinite time, arrives at is a structure of conceptual representation [*Vorstellen*] exactly like that of an infinite numerical series, infinite space, etc.

§ 5. The Transformation of Ideas through Temporal Characters

An especially important characteristic still remains to be considered with regard to Brentano's idea of time. The time-species of past and future are uniquely characterized by the fact that they do not define the elements of sensible representation with which they are combined as do other supervenient modes, but alter them. A louder tone C *is* still the tone C, and so is one that is softer. On the other hand, a tone C which *has been* is *no* tone C, a red which has been is no red. Temporal determinations do not define; they essentially alter in a manner wholly similar to determinations such as "imagined," "wished," etc. An imagined dollar, a possible dollar, *is* no dollar. Only the determination "now" is an exception. The A existing now is indeed a real A. The present does not alter, but on the other hand it also does not define. If I add "now" to the idea of man, the idea acquires no new characteristic thereby; in other words, the "now" attributes no new characteristic to the idea of man. In perception, when something is represented at present, nothing is added to the quality, intensity, or spatial determinateness thereby. The temporal predicates which qualify that to which they refer are, according to Brentano, non-real [*irreale*]; only the determination "now" is real. This involves something remarkable, namely, that non-real temporal determinations can belong in a continuous series with a unique, actual, real determinateness to which they are joined by infinitesimal differences. The real now becomes ever and again non-real. If one asks how the real is able to become non-real by being joined to qualifying temporal determinations, no answer can be given other than this: temporal determinations of every kind are joined in a certain way as necessary consequences to every instance of coming to be and passing away that takes place in the present. For, as is completely obvious and self-evident, everything that is or that becomes, in consequence of the fact that it is, *has been,* and in consequence of the fact that it is, in the future will have been.

§ 6. Critique

Turning now to a critique of the theory as presented above, we must ask first of all: What does it accomplish and what is it meant to accomplish? Obviously, it does not proceed on the basis that we recognized as necessary for a phenomenological analysis of time-consciousness. It proceeds in terms of transcendent presuppositions, with existing temporal Objects which put forth "stimuli" and "produce" sensations in us, and the like. Thus it shows itself to be a theory of the psychological origin of the idea of time. At the same time, however, it contains parts of an epistemological study concerning the conditions of the possibility of a consciousness of Objective temporality, which consciousness itself appears as temporality and must be able to so appear. To this end, there are statements concerning the characteristics of the temporal predicates which must stand in relation to psychological and phenomenological predicates. These relations, however, are not pursued further.

Brentano speaks of a law of primordial association, according to which representations of a momentary recollection are joined to particular perceptions. What is meant by this is obviously a psychological law concerning the new formation of psychical lived experiences on the basis of given psychical lived experiences. These lived experiences are psychical, they are Objectified, they themselves have their time, and the point at issue is their generation and development. Such matters belong in the sphere of psychology and do not interest us here. Nevertheless, there is a phenomenological nucleus in these observations, and the following exposition will be concerned with this exclusively. Duration, succession, and alterations appear. What is involved in this appearing? In a succession a "now" appears and, in unity therewith, a "past." The unity of the consciousness which encompasses the present and the past is a phenomenological datum. The question now is whether, as Brentano asserted, the past really appears in this consciousness in the mode of phantasy.

When Brentano speaks of gaining the future, he distinguishes between the originary intuition of time, which according to him is the creation of primordial association and extended intuition of time that arises from phantasy [3] but not from primordial association. We can also say: the intuition of time stands in contrast to the idea of time, which is unauthentic, the idea of infinite time, of temporal periods and temporal relations that are not intuitively realized. It is most extraordinary that in his theory of the intuition of time Brentano did not take into consideration the difference between the perception of time and the phantasy of time, for the difference, here obtrusive, is one that he could not possibly have overlooked. Although he was inclined to disavow talk of the perception of the temporal (with the exception of the now-point as the boundary between the past and future), the distinction which lies at the basis of the talk of the perception of succession and the calling to mind at some future time of a perceived succession (or the mere phantasy of the same) cannot be denied and must in some way be explained. If the originary intuition of time is indeed a creation of phantasy, what then distinguishes this phantasy of the temporal from that in which we are aware of a past temporal thing, a thing, therefore, that does not belong in the sphere of primordial association and that is not closed up together in one conscious-

3. "Phantasy" always includes here all presentifying [*vergegenwärtigenden*] acts and is not employed in contrast to acts of position [*setzenden Akten*]. [I use the neologism *presentify* as the translation of *vergegenwärtigen* despite the fact that the appropriate, although obsolete, term *presentiate* (to make present as in time or space) exists, because of the danger of confusing corresponding forms of *present* and *presentiate,* e.g., *presentation* and *presentiation.* J.S.C.]

ness with perception of the momentary, but was once with a past perception? If the presentification [4] of the succession lived and experienced yesterday implies a presentification of the temporal field originarily lived and experienced yesterday, and if this field manifests itself as a continuum of primordially associated phantasies, then what we now have to do with are phantasies of phantasies. Here we run up against an unresolved difficulty with regard to Brentano's theory which brings the accuracy of his analysis of originary time-consciousness into question.[5] That he was never able to overcome these difficulties lies not only in what has been said but also in other deficiencies.

Brentano did not distinguish between act and content, or between act, content of apprehension, and the object apprehended. We ourselves must be clear, however, as to where to place the temporal element. If primordial association joins a continuous sequence of ideas to the actual perception and the temporal moment is generated thereby, we must ask: What kind of temporal moment? Does it belong to the character of the act as an inherent difference essential to it or to the content of the apprehension, to the sensible content, let us say, when, for example, we consider colors and sounds in their temporal being? According to Brentano's theory, namely, that the act of representation as such does not permit differentiation, that, apart from their primary content, there is no difference between ideas as such, there is nothing left to consider but that to the primary content of perception are joined phantasms and more phantasms, qualitatively alike and differing, let us say, only in decreasing richness and intensity of content. In parallel with this, phantasy adds a new moment, the temporal. These explanations, however, are in various respects unsatisfactory. We do not encounter temporal characters such as succession and duration merely in the primary content, but also in the

4. [Cf. note 3. J.S.C.]
5. For the corresponding positive statement, cf. § 19, pp. 68ff.

Objects apprehended and in the acts of apprehension. An analysis of time which is restricted to one level is not adequate; it must rather pursue the constitution of time at all levels.

Let us ignore all transcending interpretations, however, and try to carry out the following explication with regard to the immanent content, namely, that the temporal modification is to be understood through the supervention of a moment, called the temporal moment, which is interwoven with the running-off [*Ablauf*] of the other content, with quality, intensity, and so forth. Let sound A be experienced as having just sounded and let it be renewed through primordial association and as regards its content continuously retained. This implies, however, that A (in any event, up to the weakening of its intensity) is not past but remains present. The whole difference consists in this, that the association must also be creative and add a new moment called "past." This moment grades off [*stuft sich ab*], varies continuously, and according to circumstances, A is more or less past. This implies, therefore, that the past, insofar as it falls into the sphere of the originary intuition of time, must also be present, and that the temporal moment "past" must, in the same sense as the element "red" that we actually experience, be a present moment of lived experience—which, of course, is an obvious absurdity.

One may perhaps object that, although A itself is past, a new content A with the character "past" may be in consciousness by virtue of primordial association. Nevertheless, if a similar content A is continually in consciousness, be it also with a new moment, then A is not past but present. Consequently, it is now and always present and this together with the new moment of the "past," past and present in one.—But how do we know that an A has been earlier even before the existence of the present A is past? Whence comes our idea of the past? The being-present of an A in consciousness, by means of the linking-on of a new moment (we may also call it a moment of the past), cannot be explained by the transcending consciousness by saying it is A past. Not even the slightest notion can be given of this, namely, that what I now have in consciousness as A with its new character is identical with something that is not now in consciousness but, rather, has been. What then are the moments of primordial association lived and experienced now? Are they themselves times, perhaps? If so, we are faced with the following contradiction: all these moments are there now, are enclosed in the same consciousness of objects. Therefore, they are simultaneous. But, still, the succession of time excludes their being all-at-once [Zugleich]. Are these moments, perhaps, not themselves temporal moments but rather temporal signs? But with this we have in the first place only coined a new expression. The consciousness of time is not yet analyzed. We have not yet made it clear how consciousness of something past is constituted on the basis of such signs, or in what sense, in what manner, and through what apprehensions these lived and experienced moments function otherwise than as moments of quality, and function in such a way that the reference of consciousness that a now is to be comes about through a not-now.

The attempt, therefore, to set forth what is past as something not real or not existing is very questionable. A supervenient psychical moment cannot make something non-real, or get rid of what presently exists. In fact, the whole sphere of primordial associations is a present and real lived experience. To this sphere belongs the whole series of originary temporal moments produced by means of primordial associations together with the other moments which belong to the temporal object.

We see, therefore, that it is no use to have an analysis of time-consciousness which will make the intuitive temporal interval comprehensible solely through the continuous gradation of new moments which somehow are pieced to or melted away from those moments of content which constitute the temporally localized objective entity [Gegenständliche]. To put it briefly, the form of time is itself neither the content of time nor is it a complex of new content added to the time-content in some fashion or other. If Brentano did not also fall into the error of reducing everything, after the manner of sensualism, to mere primary content, even if he was the first to recognize the radical separation between primary content and characters of acts, still his theory of time shows that he did not take into consideration the act-characters which are decisive for this theory. The question of how time-consciousness is possible and is to be understood remains unsolved.

THE ANALYSIS OF TIME-CONSCIOUSNESS

§ 7. *The Interpretation of the Comprehension of Temporal Objects* [Zeitobjekten] *as Momentary Comprehension and as Enduring Act*

A conception which derives from Herbart, was taken up by Lotze, and played a major role in the whole following period, operates as an impelling motive in Brentano's theory. The conception is this: for the comprehension of a sequence of representations (A and B, for example) it is necessary that they be the absolutely simultaneous Objects of a referential [*beziehended*] cognition which embraces them completely and indivisibly in a single unifying act. All representations of a direction, a passage, or a distance—in short, everything which includes the comparison of several elements and expresses the relation between them—can be conceived only as the product of a temporally comprehensive act of cognition. Such representations would all be impossible if the act of representation itself were completely merged in temporal succession. On this interpretation, the assumption that the intuition of a temporal interval takes place in a now, in a temporal point, appears to be self-evident and altogether inescapable. In general, it appears as a matter of course that every consciousness which concerns any whole or any plurality of distinguishable moments (therefore, every consciousness of relation and complexion) encompasses its object in an indivisible temporal point. Whenever consciousness is directed toward a whole whose parts are successive, there can be an intuitive consciousness of this whole only if the parts combine in the form of representatives [*Repräsentanten*] of the unity of the momentary intuition. Against this "dogma of the momentariness of whole of consciousness" (as he called it) W. Stern raised an objection.[6] He maintained that there are cases in which on the basis of a temporally extended content of consciousness a unitary apprehension takes place which is spread out over a temporal interval (the so-called specious present). Thus, for example, a discrete succession can be held together without prejudice to the lack of simultaneity of its members through a bond of consciousness, through a unitary apprehension. That several successive tones yield a melody is possible only in this way, that the succession of psychical processes are united "forthwith" in a common structure. They are in consciousness one after the other, but they fall within one and the same common act. We do not have the sounds all at once, as it were, and we do not hear the melody by virtue of the circumstance that the earlier tones endure with the last. Rather, the tones build up a successive unity with a common effect, the form of apprehension. Naturally, this form is perfected only with the last tone. Accordingly, there is a perception of temporally successive unities just as of coexisting ones, and, in this case, also a direct apprehension of identity, similarity, and difference. "No artificial assumption is required to the

6. "Psychische Präsenzeit," *Zeitschrift für Psychologie*, Vol. XIII (1897), pp. 325ff. Cf. also W. Stern, *Psychologie der Veränderungsaufassung* (1898).

effect that the comparison always comes about because the memory-image of the first tone always persists beside the second; rather, the entire content of consciousness uncoiling within the specious present becomes proportionate to the foundation of the resulting apprehension of similarity and difference."

What stands in the way of a clarification of the problem in dispute both in these statements and in the whole discussion associated with them is the want of the absolutely necessary distinctions which we have already portrayed in the case of Brentano. The question still remains how the apprehension of transcendent temporal Objects which extend over a duration is to be understood. Are the Objects realized in terms of a continuous similarity (like unaltered things) or as constantly changing (like material processes, motion, or alteration, for example)? Objects [*Objekte*] of this kind are constituted in a multiplicity of immanent data and apprehensions which themselves run off as a succession. Is it possible to combine these successive, expiring [*ablaufenden*], representative data in one now-moment? In that case a completely new question arises, namely, how, in addition to "temporal Objects," both immanent and transcendent, is time itself, the duration and succession of Objects, constituted? These different lines of description (which are only superficially indicated here and require further differentiation) must indeed be kept in view throughout the analysis, although all these questions are closely related so that one cannot be answered without the others.

It is indeed evident that the perception of a temporal Object itself has temporality, that perception of duration itself presupposes duration of perception, and that perception of any temporal configuration whatsoever itself has its temporal form. And, disregarding all transcendencies, the phenomenological temporality which belongs to the indispensable essence of perception according to all its phenomenological constitu-

ents still remains. Since Objective temporality is always phenomenologically constituted and is present for us as Objectivity and moment of an Objectivity according to the mode of
appearance only through this constitution, a phenomenological
analysis of time cannot explain the constitution of time without reference to the constitution of the temporal Object. By
temporal Objects, in this *particular sense,* we mean Objects
which not only are unities in time but also include temporal
extension in themselves. When a tone sounds, my Objectifying
apprehension can make the tone which endures and sounds
into an object, but not the duration of the tone or the tone
in its duration. The same also holds for a melody—for every
variation and also for every continuance considered as such.
Let us take a particular melody or cohesive part of a melody
as an example. The matter seems very simple at first; we hear
a melody, i.e., we perceive it, for hearing is indeed perception.
While the first tone is sounding, the second comes, then the
third, and so on. Must we not say that when the second tone
sounds I hear *it,* but I no longer hear the first, and so on? In
truth, therefore, I do not hear the melody but only the particular tone which is actually present. That the expired part
of the melody is objective to me is due—one is inclined to say
—to memory, and it is due to expectation which looks ahead
that, on encountering the tone actually sounding, I do not
assume that that is all.

We cannot rest satisfied with this explanation, however,
for everything said until now depends on the individual tone.
Every tone itself has a temporal extension: with the actual
sounding I hear it as now. With its continued sounding, however, it has an ever new now, and the tone actually preceding
is changing into something past. Therefore, I hear at any instant only the actual phase of the tone, and the Objectivity of
the whole enduring tone is constituted in an act-continuum
which in part is memory, in the smallest punctual part is per-

ception, and in a more extensive part expectation. However, this seems to lead back to Brentano's theory. At this point, therefore, we must initiate a more profound analysis.

§ 8. Immanent Temporal Objects [Zeitobjekte] and Their Modes of Appearance

We now exclude all transcendent apprehension and positing [Setzung] and take the sound purely as a hyletic datum. It begins and stops, and the whole unity of its duration, the unity of the whole process in which it begins and ends, "proceeds" to the end in the ever more distant past. In this sinking back, I still "hold" it fast, have it in a "retention," and as long as the retention persists the sound has its own temporality. It is the same and its duration is the same. I can direct my attention to the mode of its being given. I am conscious of the sound and the duration which it fills in a continuity of "modes," in a "continuous flux." A point, a phase of this flux is termed "consciousness of sound beginning" and therein I am conscious of the first temporal point of the duration of the sound in the mode of the now. The sound is given; that is, I am conscious of it as now, and I am so conscious of it "as long as" I am conscious of any of its phases as now. But if any temporal phase (corresponding to a temporal point of the duration of the sound) is an actual now (with the exception of the beginning point), then I am conscious of a continuity of phases as "before," and I am conscious of the whole interval of the temporal duration from the beginning-point to the now-point as an expired duration. I am not yet conscious, however, of the remaining interval of the duration. At the end-point, I am conscious of this point itself as a now-point and of the whole duration as expired (in other words, the end-point is the beginning point of a new interval of time which is no longer an interval of sound). "During" this whole flux of consciousness, I am conscious of one and the same sound as enduring, as enduring now. "Beforehand" (supposing it was not expected, for example) I was not conscious of it. "Afterward" I am "still" conscious of it "for a while" in "retention" as having been. It can be arrested and in a fixating regard [*fixierenden Blick*] be fixed and abiding. The whole interval of duration of the sound or "the" sound in its extension is something dead, so to speak, a no longer living production, a structure animated by no productive point of the now. This structure, however, is continually modified and sinks back into emptiness [*Leere*]. The modification of the entire interval then is an analogous one, essentially identical with that modification which, during the period of actuality, the expired portion of the duration undergoes in the passage of consciousness to ever new productions.

What we have described here is the manner in which the immanent-temporal Object "appears" in a continuous flux, i.e., how it is "given." To describe this manner does not mean to describe the temporal duration itself, for it is the same sound with its duration that belongs to it, which, although not described, to be sure, is presupposed in the description. The same duration is present, actual, self-generating duration and then is past, "expired" duration, still known or produced in recollection "as if" it were new. The same sound which is heard now is, from the point of view of the flux of consciousness which follows it, past, its duration expired. To my consciousness, points of temporal duration recede, as points of a stationary object in space recede when I "go away from the object." The object retains its place; even so does the sound retain its time. Its temporal point is unmoved, but the sound vanishes into the remoteness of consciousness; the distance from the generative now becomes ever greater. The sound itself is the same, but "in the way that" it appears, the sound is continually different.

§ 9. The Consciousness of the Appearances of Immanent Objects [Objekte]

On closer inspection, we are able to distinguish still other lines of thought with reference to the description: (1) We can make self-evident assertions concerning the immanent Object in itself, e.g., that it now endures, that a certain part of the duration has elapsed, that the duration of the sound apprehended in the now (naturally, with the content of the sound) constantly sinks back into the past and an ever new point of duration enters into the now or is now, that the expired duration recedes from the actual now-point (which is continually filled up in some way or other) and moves back into an ever more "distant" past, and so on. (2) We can also speak of the way in which we are "conscious of" all differences in the "appearing" of immanent sounds and their content of duration. We speak here with reference to the perception of the duration of the sound which extends into the actual now, and say that the sound, which endures, is perceived, and that of the interval of duration of the sound only the point of duration characterized as now is veritably perceived. Of the interval that has expired we say that we are conscious of it in retentions, specifically, that we are conscious of those parts or phases of the duration, not sharply to be differentiated, which lie closest to the actual now-point with diminishing clarity, while those parts lying further back in the past are wholly unclear; we are conscious of them only as empty [leer]. The same thing is true with regard to the running-off of the entire duration. Depending on its distance from the actual now, that part of the duration which lies closest still has perhaps a little clarity; the whole disappears in obscurity, in a void retentional consciousness, and finally disappears completely (if one may say so) as soon as retention ceases.[7]

7. It is tempting to draw a parallel between these modes of the consciousness and appearance of temporal Objects and the modes in which a spatial thing appears and is known with changing orientation, to

In the clear sphere we find, therefore, a greater distinction and dispersion (in fact, the more so, the closer the sphere to the actual now). The further we withdraw from the now, however, the greater the blending and drawing together. If in reflection we immerse ourselves in the unity of a structured process, we observe that an articulated part of the process "draws together" as it sinks into the past—a kind of temporal perspective (within the originary temporal appearance) analogous to spatial perspective. As the temporal Object moves into the past, it is drawn together on itself and thereby also becomes obscure.

We must now examine more closely what we find here and can describe as the phenomena of temporally constitutive consciousness, that consciousness in which temporal objects with their temporal determinations are constituted. We distinguish the enduring, immanent Object in its modal setting [*das Objekt im Wie*], the way in which we are conscious of it as actually present or as past. Every temporal being "appears" in one or another continually changing mode of running-off, and the "Object in the mode of running-off" is in this change always something other, even though we still say that the Object and every point of its time and this time itself are one and the same. The "Object in the mode of running-off" we cannot term a form of consciousness (any more than we can call a spatial phenomenon, a body in its appearance from one side or the other, from far or near, a form of consciousness). "Consciousness," "lived experience," refers to an Object by means of an appearance in which "the Object in its modal setting" subsists. Obviously, we must recognize talk of "intentionality" as ambiguous, depending on whether we have in mind the relation of the appearance to what appears or the relation of consciousness on the one hand to "what appears

pursue further the "temporal orientations" in which spatial things (which are also temporal Objects) appear. Yet, for the time being, we shall remain in the immanent sphere.

in its modal setting" and on the other to what merely appears.

§ 10. The Continua of Running-off Phenomena
—The Diagram of Time

We should prefer to avoid talk of "appearance" when referring to phenomena which constitute temporal Objects, for these phenomena are themselves immanent Objects and are appearances in a wholly different sense. We speak here of "running-off phenomena" [Ablaufsphänomene], or better yet of "modes of temporal orientation," and with reference to the immanent Objects themselves of their "running-off characters" (e.g., now, past). With regard to the running-off phenomenon, we know that it is a continuity of constant transformations which form an inseparable unit, not severable into parts which could be by themselves nor divisible into phases, points of the continuity, which could be by themselves. The parts which by a process of abstraction we can throw into relief can be only in the entire running-off. This is also true of the phases and points of the continuity of running-off. It is evident that we can also say of this continuity that in certain ways it is unalterable as to form. It is unthinkable that the continuity of phases would be such that it contained the same phase-mode twice or indeed contained it extended over an entire part-interval. Just as every temporal point (and every temporal interval) is, so to speak, different from every other "individual" point and cannot occur twice, so also no mode of running-off can occur twice. However, we shall carry our analysis still further here and hence must make our distinctions clear.

To begin with, we emphasize that modes of running-off of an immanent temporal Object have a beginning, that is to say, a source-point. This is the mode of running-off with which the immanent Object begins to be. It is characterized as now. In the continuous line of advance, we find something remarkable, namely, that every subsequent phase of running-off is itself a continuity, and one constantly expanding, a continuity of pasts. The continuity of the modes of running-off of the duration of the Object we contrast to the continuity of the modes of running-off of each point of the duration which obviously is enclosed in the continuity of

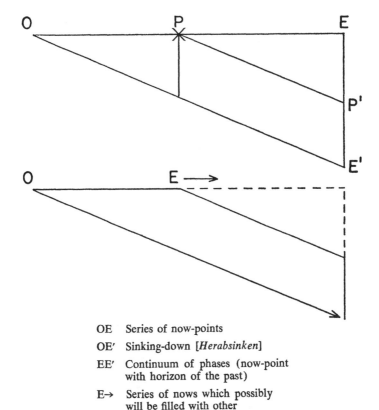

OE   Series of now-points

OE′   Sinking-down [*Herabsinken*]

EE′   Continuum of phases (now-point with horizon of the past)

E→   Series of nows which possibly will be filled with other Objects

those first modes of running-off; therefore, the continuity of running-off of an enduring Object is a continuum whose phases are the continua of the modes of running-off of the different temporal points of the duration of the Object. If we go along the concrete continuity, we advance in continuous modifications, and in this process the mode of running-off is constantly modified, i.e., along the continuity of running-off of the temporal points concerned. Since a new now is always presenting itself, each now is changed into a past, and thus the entire continuity of the running-off of the pasts of the preceding points moves uniformly "downward" into the depths of the past. In our figure the solid horizontal line illustrates the modes of running-off of the enduring Object. These modes extend from a point O on for a definite interval which has the last now as an end-point. Then the series of modes of running-off begins which no longer contains a now (of this duration). The duration is no longer actual but past and constantly sinks deeper into the past. The figure thus provides a complete picture of the double continuity of modes of running-off.

§ 11. Primal Impression and Retentional Modification

The "source-point" with which the "generation" of the enduring Object begins is a primal impression. This consciousness is engaged in continuous alteration. The actual [leibhafte] tonal now is constantly changed into something that has been; constantly, an ever fresh tonal now, which passes over into modification, peels off. However, when the tonal now, the primal impression, passes over into retention, this retention is itself again a now, an actual existent. While it itself is actual (but not an actual sound), it is the retention of a sound that has been. A ray of meaning [Strahl der Meinung] can be directed toward the now, toward the retention, but it can also be directed toward that of which we are conscious in retention, the past sound. Every actual now of consciousness, however, is subject to the law of modification. The now changes continuously from retention to retention. There results, therefore, a stable continuum which is such that every subsequent point is a retention for every earlier one. And every retention is already a continuum. The sound begins and steadily continues. The tonal now is changed into one that has been. Constantly flowing, the *impressional* consciousness passes over into an ever fresh *retentional* consciousness. Going along the flux or with it, we have a continuous series of retentions pertaining to the beginning point. Moreover, every earlier point of this series shades off [*sich abschattet*] again as a now in the sense of retention. Thus, in each of these retentions is included a continuity of retentional modifications, and this continuity is itself again a point of actuality which retentionally shades off. This does not lead to a simple infinite regress because each retention is in itself a continuous modification which, so to speak, bears in itself the heritage [*Erbe*] of the past in the form of a series of shadings. It is not true that lengthwise along the flux each earlier retention is merely replaced by a new one, even though it is a continuous process. Each subsequent retention, rather, is not merely a continuous modification arising from the primal impression but a continuous modification of the same beginning point.

Up to this point, we have been chiefly concerned with the perception of the originary constitution of temporal Objects and have sought analytically to understand the consciousness of time given in them. However, the consciousness of temporality does not take place merely in this form. When a temporal Object has expired, when its actual duration is over, the consciousness of the Object, now past, by no means fades away, although it no longer functions as perceptual consciousness, or better, perhaps, as impressional consciousness. (As before, we have in mind immanent Objects, which are not really constituted in a "perception.") To the "impression," "primary remembrance" [*primäre Erinnerung*], or, as we say, retention, is joined. Basically, we have already analyzed this mode of consciousness in conjunction with the situation previously considered. For the continuity of phases joined to the actual "now" is indeed nothing other than such a retention or a continuity of retentions. In the case of the perception of a temporal Object (it makes no difference to the present observation whether we take an immanent or transcendent Object), the perception always terminates in a now-apprehension, in a perception in the sense of a positing-as-now. During the perception of motion there takes place, moment by moment, a "comprehension-as-now;" constituted therein is the now actual phase of the motion itself. But this now-apprehension is, as it were, the nucleus of a comet's tail of retentions referring to the earlier now-points of the motion. If perception no longer occurs, however, we no longer see motion, or—if it is a question of a melody—the melody is over and silence begins. Thus no new phase is joined to the last phase; rather, we have a mere phase of fresh memory, to this is again joined another such, and so on. There continually takes place, thereby, a shoving back into the past. The same complex continuously undergoes a modification until it disappears, for hand in hand with the modification goes a diminution which finally ends in imperceptibility. The originary temporal field is obviously circumscribed exactly like a perceptual one. Indeed, generally speaking, one might well venture the assertion that the temporal field always has the same extension. It is displaced, as it were, with regard to the perceived and freshly remembered motion and its Objective time in a manner similar to the way in which the visual field is displaced with regard to Objective space.[8]

§ 12. Retention as Proper Intentionality

We must still discuss in greater detail what sort of modification it is that we designate as retentional.

One speaks of the dying or fading away, etc., of the con-

8. No notice is taken in the diagram of the limitation of the temporal field. No end to retention is provided for therein, and, ideally

tent of sensation when veritable perception passes over into retention. Now, according to the statements made hitherto, it is already clear that the retentional "content" is, in the primordial sense, no content at all. When a sound dies away, it is first sensed with particular fullness (intensity), and thereupon comes to an end in a sudden reduction of intensity. The sound is still there, is still sensed, but in mere reverberation. This real sensation of sound should be distinguished from the tonal moment in retention. The retentional sound is not actually present but "primarily remembered" precisely in the now. It is not really on hand in retentional consciousness. The tonal moment that belongs to this consciousness, however, cannot be another sound which is really on hand, not even a very weak one which is qualitatively similar (like an echo). A present sound can indeed remind us of a past sound, present it, symbolize it; this, however, already presupposes another representation of the past. The intuition of the past itself cannot be a symbolization [*Verbildlichung*]; it is an originary consciousness. Naturally, we cannot deny that echoes exist. But where we recognize and distinguish them we are soon able to establish that they do not belong to retention as such but to perception. The reverberation of a violin tone is a very weak violin tone and is completely different from the retention of loud sounds which have just been. The reverberation itself, as well as after-images in general, which remain behind after the stronger givens of sensation, has absolutely nothing to do with the nature of retention, to say nothing of the possibility that the reverberation must necessarily be ascribed to retention.

Truly, however, it pertains to the essence of the intuition of time that in every point of its duration (which, reflectively, we are able to make into an object) it is consciousness of *what has*

at least, a form of consciousness is possible in which everything is retentionally retained.

With regard to the foregoing, cf. Appendix I, pp. 129ff.

just been and not mere consciousness of the now-point of the objective thing appearing as having duration. In this consciousness, we are aware of what has just been in the continuity pertaining to it and in every phase in a determinate "mode of appearance" differentiated as to "content" and "apprehension." One notices the steam whistle just sounding; in every point there is an extension and in the extension there is the "appearance" which, in every phase of this extension, has its moment of quality and its moment of apprehension. On the other hand, the moment of quality is no real quality, no sound which really is now, i.e., which exists as now, provided that one can speak of the immanent content of sound. The real content of the now-consciousness includes sounds which, if the occasion should arise, are sensed; in which case, they are then necessarily to be characterized in Objectifying apprehension as perceived, as present, but in no wise as past. Retentional consciousness includes real consciousness of the past of sound, primary remembrance of sound, and is not to be resolved into sensed sound and apprehension as memory. Just as a phantasied sound is not a sound but the phantasy of a sound, or just as tonal sensation and tonal phantasy are fundamentally different and are not to be considered as possibly the same, except for a difference in interpretation, likewise primary, intuitive remembered sound is intrinsically something other than a perceived sound, and the primary remembrance of sound is something other than the sensation of sound.

§ 13. *The Necessity for the Precedence of Impression over Every Retention—Self-evidence of Retention*

Is there a law to the effect that primary remembrance is possible only if continuously joined to a preceding sensation or perception, that every retentional phase is thinkable only as a phase, i.e., is not to be expanded into an interval which would be identical in all phases? One might say without reservation that this is absolutely evident. An empirical psychologist, accustomed to treating everything psychical as a mere succession of events, would of course deny this. Such a person would say: Why should not an originative [*anfangendes*] consciousness be thinkable, one which begins with a fresh remembrance without previously having had a perception? It may in fact be the case that perception is necessary to produce a fresh remembrance. It may actually be true that human consciousness can have memories, primary ones included, only after it has had perceptions, but the opposite is also conceivable. In contrast to this, we teach the *a priori* necessity of the precedence of a perception or primal impression over the corresponding retention. We must above all insist that a phase is thinkable only as a phase and without the possibility of an extension. A now-phase is thinkable only as the boundary of a continuity of retentions, just as every retentional phase is itself thinkable only as a point of such a continuum, that is, for every now of the consciousness of time. If this is true, however, an entire completed series of retentions should not be thinkable without a corresponding perception preceding it. This implies that the series of retentions which pertains to a now is itself a limit and is necessarily modified. What is remembered "sinks ever further into the past;" moreover, what is remembered is necessarily something sunken, something that of necessity permits an evident recollection [*Wiedererinnerung*] which traces it back to a now reproduced.

One might ask, however: Can I not have a memory, even a primary one, of an A which in truth has never existed? Certainly. Something even stronger can be asserted. I can also have a perception of A although in reality A does not exist. Accordingly, we do not assert as a certainty that when we have a retention of A (assuming A is a transcendent Object), A must precede the retention, although we do assert that A must have been perceived.

Whether A is the object of primary attention or not, it really is present as something of which we are conscious even if unnoticed or noticed only incidentally. If it is a question of an immanent Object, however, the following holds true: a succession, an alternation, a variation of immanent data, if it "appears," is absolutely indubitable. And within a transcendent perception, the immanent succession belonging essentially to the composition of this perception is also absolutely indubitable.[9] It is *basically absurd* to argue: How in the now can I know of a not-now, since I cannot compare the not-now which no longer is with the now (that is to say, the memory-image present in the now)? As if it pertained to the essence of memory that an image present in the now were presupposed for another thing similar to it, and as with graphic representation, I could and must compare the two. Memory or retention is not figurative consciousness, but something totally different. What is remembered *is,* of course, not now; otherwise it would not be something that has been but would be actually present. And in memory (retention) what is remembered is not given as now: otherwise, memory or retention would not be just memory but perception (or primal impression). A comparison of what we no longer perceive but are merely conscious of in retention with something outside it makes no sense at all. Just as in perception, I see what has being now, and in extended perceptions, no matter how constituted, what has enduring being, so in primary remembrance I see what is past. What is past is given therein, and givenness of the past is memory.

If we now again take up the question of whether a retentional consciousness that is not the continuation of an impressional consciousness is thinkable, we must say that it is impossible, for every retention in itself refers back to an impres-

9. Cf. also the distinction between internal and external perception, § 44, pp. 122ff.

sion. "Past" and "now" exclude each other. Something past and something now can indeed be identically the same but only because it has endured between the past and now.

§ 14. Reproduction of Temporal Objects [Objekten]—Secondary Remembrance

We characterized primary remembrance or retention as a comet's tail which is joined to actual perception. Secondary remembrance or recollection is completely different from this. After primary remembrance is past [dahin], a new memory of this motion or that melody can emerge. The difference between the two forms of memory, which we have already touched on, must now be explained in detail. If retention is joined to actual perception, whether during its perceptual flux or in continuous union following its running-off, then at first sight it is natural to say (as Brentano has) that the actual perception is constituted on the basis of phantasies as representation [Repräsentation], as presentification. Now, just as immediate presentifications are joined to perceptions, so also can autonomous presentifications appear without being joined to perceptions. Such are the secondary remembrances. But (as we have already brought out in the critique of Brentano's theory) serious doubts arise. Let us consider an example of secondary remembrance. We remember a melody, let us say, which in our youth we heard during a concert. Then it is obvious that the entire phenomenon of memory has, *mutatis mutandis,* exactly the same constitution as the perception of the melody. Like the perception, it has a favored point; to the now-point of the perception corresponds a now-point of the memory, and so on. We run through a melody in phantasy; we hear "as if" [gleichsam] first the first note, then the second, etc. At any given time, there is always a sound (or a tonal phase) in the now-point. The preceding sounds, however, are

57

not erased from consciousness. With the apprehension of the sound appearing now, heard as if now, primary remembrance blends in the sounds heard as if just previously and the expectation (protention) of the sound to come. Again, the now-point has for consciousness a temporal halo [*Hof*] which is brought about through a continuity of memory. The complete memory of the melody consists of a continuum of such temporal continuities or of continuities of apprehension of the kind described. Finally, when the melody presentified has been run through, a retention is joined to this as-if hearing; the as-if heard still reverberates a while, a continuity of apprehension is still there but no longer as heard. Everything thus resembles perception and primary remembrance and yet is not itself perception and primary remembrance. We do not really hear and have not really heard when in memory or phantasy we let a melody run its course, note by note. In the former case, we really hear; the temporal Object itself is perceived; the melody itself is the object of perception. And, likewise, temporal periods, temporal determinations and relations are themselves given, perceived. And again, after the melody has sounded, we no longer perceive it as present although we still have it in consciousness. It is no longer a present melody but one just past. Its being just past is not mere opinion but a given fact, self-given and therefore perceived. In contrast to this, the temporal present [*Gegenwart*] in recollection is remembered, presentified. And the past is remembered in the same way, presentified but not perceived. It is not the primarily given and intuited past.

On the other hand, the recollection itself is present, originarily constituted recollection and subsequently that which has just been. It generates itself in a continuum of primal data and retentions and is constituted (better, re-constituted) jointly with an immanent or transcendent objectivity of duration (depending on whether it is immanently or transcendently oriented). On the other hand, retention generates no objectivities of duration (whether originary or reproductive), but merely retains what is produced in consciousness and impresses on it the character of the "just past." [10]

§ 15. The Modes of Accomplishment of Reproduction

Recollection can make its appearance in different forms of accomplishment. We accomplish it either by simply laying hold of what is recollected, as when, for example, a recollection "emerges" and we look at what is remembered with a glancing ray [*Blickstrahl*] wherein what is remembered is indeterminate, perhaps a favored momentary phase intuitively brought forth, but not a recapitulative memory. Or we accomplish it in a real, re-productive, recapitulative memory in which the temporal object is again completely built up in a continuum of presentifications, so that we seem to perceive it again, but only seemingly, as-if. The whole process is a presentificational modification of the process of perception with all its phases and levels, including retentions. However, everything has the index of reproductive modification.

The simple act of looking at or apprehending we also discover immediately on the basis of retention, as, for example, when a melody which lies within the unity of a retention is run through and we look back (reflect) on a part of it without producing it again. This is an act which, developed in successive stages, also in stages of spontaneity, e.g., the spontaneity of thought, is possible for everyone. The objectivities of thought, indeed, are also successively constituted. It appears, therefore, we can say that objectivities which are built up originally in temporal processes, being constituted member by member or phase by phase (as correlates of continuous, multiformed, cohesive, and homogenous acts), may be

10. For a discussion of further differences between retention and reproduction, cf. § 19, pp. 68ff.

apprehended in a backward glance as if they were objects complete in a temporal point. But then this givenness certainly refers back to another "primordial" one.

This looking toward or back to what is retentionally given —and the retention itself—is realized in true representification [*Wiedervergegenwärtigung*]. What is given as just having been turns out to be identical with what is recollected.

Further differences between primary and secondary remembrance will be evident when we relate them to perception.

§ 16. Perception as Originary Presentation [Gegenwärtigung] *as Distinguished from Retention and Recollection*

Any reference to "perception" still requires some discussion here. In the "perception of a melody," we distinguish the tone *given now,* which we term the "perceived," from those which *have gone by,* which we say are "not perceived." On the other hand, we call the *whole melody* one that is *perceived,* although only the now-point actually is. We follow this procedure because not only is the extension of the melody given point for point in an extension of the act of perception but also the unity of retentional consciousness still "holds" the expired tones themselves in consciousness and continuously establishes the unity of consciousness with reference to the homogeneous temporal Object, i.e., the melody. An Objectivity such as a melody cannot itself be originarily given except as "perceived" in this form. The constituted act,[11] constructed from now-consciousness and retentional consciousness, is *adequate perception of the temporal Object.* This Object will indeed include temporal differences, and temporal differences are constituted precisely in such phases, in primal consciousness, retention, and protention. If the pur-

11. Concerning acts as constituted unities in primordial consciousness, cf. § 37, pp. 100ff.

posive [*meinende*] intention is directed toward the melody, toward the whole Object, we have nothing but perception. If the intention is directed toward a particular tone or a particular measure for its own sake, we have perception so long as precisely the thing intended is perceived, and mere retention as soon as it is past. Objectively [*objektiver*] considered, the measure no longer appears as "present" but as "past." The whole melody, however, appears as present so long as it still sounds, so long as the notes *belonging to it,* intended in the *one* nexus of apprehensions, still sound. The melody is past only after the last note has gone.

As we must assert in accordance with the preceding statements, *this relativation* carries over to the individual *tones.* Each is constituted in a continuity of tonal data, and only a punctual phase is actually present as now at any given moment, while the others are connected as a retentional train. We can say, however, that a temporal Object is perceived (or intentionally known) as long as it is still produced in continuous, newly appearing primal impressions.

We have then characterized *the past* itself as perceived. If, in fact, we do not perceive *the passing* [*Vergehen*], are we not, in the cases described, directly conscious of the *just-having-been* of the "just past" in its self-givenness, in the mode of *being self-given*? Obviously, the meaning of "perception" here obtaining does not coincide with the earlier one. Further analysis is required.

If, in the comprehension of a temporal Object, we distinguish between perceptive and memorial [*erinnerendes*] (retentional) consciousness, then the contrast between the perception and the primary remembrance of an Object corresponds to that between "now present" and "past." *Temporal Objects,* and this belongs to their essence, spread their content over an *interval of time,* and such Objects can be constituted only in acts which likewise constitute temporal distinctions. Temporally constitutive acts, however, are essentially acts which also constitute the present and the past. They have that type of "temporal Object-perception" which, in conformity with their peculiar apprehensional constitution, we have described in detail. Temporal Objects must be thus constituted. This implies that an act which claims to give a temporal Object itself must contain in itself "now-apprehensions," "past-apprehensions," and the like, and, in fact, in a primordially constitutive way.

If we now relate what has been said about perception to the *differences of the givenness* with which temporal Objects make their appearance, then the *antithesis of perception* is *primary remembrance,* which appears here, and *primary expectation* (retention and protention), whereby *perception and non-perception continually* pass over into one another. In the consciousness of the direct, intuitive comprehension of a temporal Object, e.g., a melody, the passage, tone, or part now heard is perceived, and not perceived is what is momentarily intuited as past. Apprehensions here pass continually over into one another and terminate in an apprehension constituting the now; this apprehension, however, is only an ideal limit. We are concerned here with a *continuum of gradations in the direction of an ideal limit,* like the convergence of various shades of red toward an ideally pure red. However, in this case, we do not have individual apprehensions corresponding to the individual shades of red, which, indeed, *can be given for themselves.* Rather, we always have and, according to the nature of the matter, can only have continuities of apprehensions, or better, *a single continuum which is constantly modified.* If somehow we divide this continuum into two adjoining parts, that part which includes the now, or is capable of constituting it, designates and constitutes the "gross" now, which, as soon as we divide it further, immediately breaks down again into a finer now and a past, etc.

Perception, therefore, has here the character of an act which includes a continuity of such characters and is distinguished by the possession of that ideal limit mentioned above. Pure memory is a similar continuity, but one which does not possess this ideal limit. In an ideal sense, then, perception (impression) would be the phase of consciousness which constitutes the pure now, and memory every other phase of the continuity. But this is just an ideal limit, something abstract which can be nothing for itself. Moreover, it is also true that even this ideal now is not something *toto caelo* different from the not-now but continually accommodates itself thereto. The continual transition from perception to primary remembrance conforms to this accommodation.

§ 17. Perception as a Self-Giving [Selbstgebender] Act in Contrast to Reproduction

Perception, or the self-giving of the actual present, which has its correlate in the given of what is past, is now confronted by another contrast, that of recollection, secondary remembrance. In recollection, a now "appears" to us, but it "appears" in a sense wholly other than the appearance of the now in perception.[12] This now *is not perceived, i.e., self-given, but presentified.* It places a now before us which is not given. In just the same way, the running-off of a melody in *recollection* places before us a "just past," but does not give it. In addition, every individual in mere phantasy is temporally extended in some way. It has its now, its before and after [*sein vorher und Nachher*], but like the whole Object, the now, before, and after are merely imagined. Here, therefore, it is a question of an *entirely different concept of perception.* Here, *perception* is an act which brings something *other than itself before us,* an act which *primordially constitutes* the Object. *Presentification,* re-presentation, as the act which does not place an

12. Cf. Appendix II: Presentification and Phantasy—Impression and Imagination, pp. 133ff.

Object itself before us, but just presentifies—places before us in images, as it were (if not precisely in the manner of true figurative consciousness)—, is just the opposite of this. There is no mention here of a continuous accommodation of perception to its opposite. Heretofore, consciousness of the past, i.e., the primary one, was not perception because perception was designated as the act originarily constituting the now. Consciousness of the past, however, does not constitute a now but rather a *"just-having-been"* [*ein soeben gewesen*] that intuitively precedes the now. However, if we call perception *the act in which all "origination" lies*, which *constitutes originarily,* then *primary remembrance is perception.* For only in *primary remembrance do we see what is past;* only in it is the past constituted, i.e., *not in a representative but in a presentative way.* The just-having-been, the before in contrast to the now, can be seen directly only in primary remembrance. It is the essence of primary remembrance to bring this new and unique moment to primary, direct intuition, just as it is the essence of the perception of the now to bring the now directly to intuition. On the other hand, recollection, like phantasy, offers us mere presentification. It is "as-if" the same consciousness as the temporarily creative acts of the now and the past, "as-if" the same but yet modified. The phantasied now represents a now, but does not give us a now itself; the phantasied before and after merely represents a before and after, etc.

§ 18. The Significance of Recollection for the Constitution of the Consciousness of Duration and Succession

The constitutive significance of primary and secondary remembrance is seen in a different light if, instead of the mode of givenness of *enduring objectivities,* we turn our attention to the mode of givenness of *duration* and *succession* themselves.

Let us suppose that A appears as a primal impression and endures for a while, and along with the retention of A in a certain level of development B appears and is constituted as enduring B. Therewith, during these "processes," consciousness is consciousness of the same A "moving back into the past," the same A in the flux of these modes of givenness, and the same according to the "duration" belonging to the form of being appropriate to its content according to all points of this duration. The same is true of B and of the difference of both durations or their temporal points. In addition to the above, however, something new enters here: *B follows A.* There is a succession of two continuing sets of data given with a determinate temporal form, a temporal interval which encompasses the succession. The *consciousness of succession* is an originary dator [*gebendes*] consciousness; it is the "perception" of this succession. We shall consider now the reproductive modification of this perception, that is, recollection. I "repeat" *the consciousness of this succession:* remembering, I presentify it to myself. This I *"can"* do, in fact, as "often as I like." The presentification of a lived experience lies *a priori* within the sphere of my "freedom." (The "I can" is a practical "I can" and not a "mere idea.") Now what does the presentification of a lived experience look like and what belongs to its essence? One can say to begin with: I presentify to myself first A and then B. If I originally have A—B, now I have A'—B' (the mark ['] indicates memory). But this is inadequate, for it implies that I now have a memory A' and "afterward" a memory B', namely, in the consciousness of a succession of these memories. But then I should have a "perception" of the succession of these memories and no consciousness of the memory of them. I must therefore exhibit this consciousness through (A—B)'. This consciousness, in

65

fact, includes an A′, B′, and also a —. To be sure, the succession is not a third part, as if the manner of writing down the signs one after the other denoted the succession. Nevertheless, I can write down the law

$$(A{-}B)' = A'{-}B'$$

meaning: there is present a consciousness of the memory of A and of B but also a modified consciousness of "B follows A."

If, as regards the originary dator consciousness, we now ask for a succession of enduring Objectivities—and, indeed, for the duration itself—we find that retention and recollection necessarily belong thereto. Retention constitutes the living horizon of the now; I have in it a consciousness of the "just past." But what is originarily constituted thereby—perhaps in the retaining of the tone just heard—is only the shoving back of the now-phase or the completed constituted duration, which in this completeness is no longer being constituted and no longer perceived. In "coincidence" with this "result" which is being shoved back, I can, however, undertake a reproduction. Then the pastness [*Vergangenheit*] of the duration is given to me *simpliciter* as just is the "re-givenness" [*Wiedergegebenheit*] of the duration. And it should be noted that it is only past durations that I can, in repeatable acts, "originarily" intuit, identify, and have objectively as the identical Object of many acts. I can re-live [*nachleben*] the present but it can never be given again. If I come back to one and the same succession (as I can at any time) and identify it as the same temporal Object, I carry out a succession of recollective lived experiences in the unity of an overlapping consciousness of succession thus:

$$(A{-}B){-}(A{-}B)'{-}(A{-}B)''. \ . \ . \ .$$

The question is: what is this act of identification like? To begin with, the succession is a succession of lived experiences —the first being the originary constitution of a succession

A—B, the second a memory of this succession, then the same thing again, and so on. The entire succession is given originarily as presence [*Präsenz*]. I can again have a memory of this succession, another memory of such a recollection, and so on *ad infinitum*. Essentially, every memory is not only repeatable in the sense that higher levels are possible at will, but also it is repeated as a sphere of the "I can."

What is the first recollection of that succession like? It is:

$$[(A\text{—}B)\text{—}(A\text{—}B)']'$$

Then, according to the earlier law, I can deduce that therein is set $(A\text{—}B)'$ and $[(A\text{—}B)']'$, therefore, a memory of the second level, that is, in the sequence, and naturally also the memory of the succession —'. If I repeat once again, I have still higher modifications of memory and at the same time the consciousness that in sequence I have again and again carried out a repeatable presentification. Such a thing takes place very often. I knock twice on the table and presentify the sequence to myself. Then I note that I first gave the succession perceptively and then remembered it. Then I note that I have accomplished just this noting, that is, as the third member of a series that I can repeat, etc. This is all very commonplace, especially in the phenomenological method of procedure.

In the succession of like Objects (identical as to content) which are given only in succession and never as coexisting, we have a peculiar coincidence in the unity of one consciousness. Naturally, this is meant only figuratively, for the Objects are indeed separated, known as a succession, divided by a temporal interval.

And yet, we have in the sequence unlike Objects, with like contrasted moments. Thus "lines of likeness," as it were, run from one to the other, and in the case of similarity, lines of similarity. We have an interrelatedness which is not constituted in a relational mode of observation and which is prior to all "comparison" and all "thinking" as the necessary condition for all intuition of likeness and difference. Only the similar is really "comparable" and "difference" presupposes "coincidence," i.e., that real union of the like bound together in transition (or in coexistence).

§ 19. The Difference between Retention and Reproduction (Primary and Secondary Remembrance or Phantasy)

By this time our position regarding Brentano's theory that the origin of the apprehension of time lies in the sphere of phantasy is definitely determined. Phantasy is the mode of consciousness characterized as presentification (reproduction). Now, there is indeed such a thing as presentified time but it necessarily refers back to a primordially given time which is not phantasied but presented. Presentification is the opposite of the primordially giving act; no representation can arise from it. That is, phantasy is not a form of consciousness that can bring forth some kind of Objectivity or other, or an essential and possible tendency [Zug] toward an Objectivity as self-given. Not to be self-giving is precisely the essence of phantasy. Even the concept of phantasy does not arise from phantasy. For if we claim originarily to have given what phantasy is, then we must, of course, form phantasies, but this itself still does not mean givenness. We must naturally observe the process of phantasy, i.e., perceive it. The perception of phantasy is the primordially giving consciousness for the formation of the concept of phantasy. In this perception, we see what phantasy is; we grasp it in the consciousness of self-givenness.

That a great phenomenological difference exists between representifying memory and primary remembrance which extends the now-consciousness is revealed by a careful comparison of the lived experiences involved in both. We hear, let us say, two or three sounds and have during the temporal extension of the now a consciousness of the sound just heard.

Evidently this consciousness is essentially the same whether out of the tonal configuration which forms the unity of a temporal Object a member is still really perceived as now, or whether this member no longer occurs, although we are still retentionally aware of the image. Let us assume now that it perhaps happens that while the continuous intention directed toward the sound or flow of the sound is still vivid, this same sound is reproduced once more. The measure which I have just heard and toward which my attention is still directed I presentify to myself in that inwardly I carry it out once more. The difference is obvious. In the presentification we now once more have the sound or sound-form together with its entire temporal extension. The act of presentification has exactly the same temporal extension as the earlier act of perception. The former reproduces the latter; it allows the passage to run off, tonal phase for tonal phase and interval for interval. It also reproduces thereby the phase of primary remembrance which we have singled out for the comparison. Nevertheless, the act of presentification is not a mere repetition and the difference does not merely consist in that at the one time we have a simple reproduction and at the other a reproduction of a reproduction. We find, rather, radical differences in content. They become apparent when, for example, we inquire what constitutes the difference between the sounding of the tone in the presentification and in the residual consciousness of it which we still retain in phantasy. The tone reproduced during the "sounding" is a reproduction of the sounding. The residual consciousness after the sounding has been reproduced is no longer a reproduction of the sounding but of the re-sounding [Er-klingens] which has just been but is still heard. This re-sounding is exhibited in an entirely different manner from that of the sounding itself. The phantasms which exhibit the tones do not remain in consciousness as if, for example, in the presentification each tone were constituted as an identical persisting datum. Otherwise, in presentification we could not have an intuitive idea of time, the idea of a temporal Object. The tone reproduced passes away; its phantasm does not remain identically the same, but is modified in a characteristic way and establishes the presentificational consciousness of duration, alteration, succession, and the like.

The modification of consciousness which changes an originary now into one that is *reproduced* is something wholly other than that modification which changes the now—whether originary or reproduced—into the *past*. This last modification has the character of a continuous shading-off; just as the now continuously grades off into the ever more distant past, so the intuitive consciousness of time also continuously grades off. On the other hand, we are not speaking here of a continuous transition of perception to phantasy, of impression to reproduction. The latter distinction is a separate one. We must say, therefore, that what we term originary consciousness, impression, or perception is an act which is continuously gradated. Every concrete perception implies a whole continuum of such gradations. Reproduction, phantasy-consciousness, also requires exactly the same gradations, although only reproductively modified. On both sides, it belongs to the essence of lived experiences that they must be extended in this fashion, that a punctual phase can never be for itself.

Naturally, the gradation of what is given originarily as well as of what is given reproductively indeed concerns the content of apprehension, as we have already seen. Perception is built upon sensations. Sensation which functions presentatively for the object forms a stable continuum, and in just the same way the phantasm forms a continuum for the representation [*Repräsentation*] of an Object of phantasy. Whoever assumes an essential difference between sensations and phantasms naturally may not claim the content of apprehension of the temporal phases just past to be phantasms, for these, of course, pass continually over into the content of apprehension of the moment of the now.

§ 20. The "Freedom" of Reproduction

In the originary and the reproductive running-off of "sinking-back" noteworthy differences appear. The originary appearing and passing away of the modes of running-off in appearance is something fixed, something of which we are conscious through "affection," something we can only observe (if, in general, we achieve the spontaneity of such viewing). On the other hand, presentification is something free; it is a free running-through [*Durchlaufen*]. We can carry out the presentification "more quickly" or "more slowly," clearly and explicitly or in a confused manner, quick as lightning at a stroke or in articulated steps, and so on. Presentification is thus itself an occurrence of internal consciousness and as such has its actual now, its modes of running-off, etc. And in the same immanent temporal interval in which the presentification really takes place, we can "in freedom" accommodate larger and smaller parts of the presentified event with its modes of running-off and consequently run through it more quickly or more slowly. Thereby, the relative modes of running-off (under the presupposition of a continuous identifying coincidence) of the points of the temporal interval presentified remain unchanged. I always presentify the same, always the same continuity of the modes of running-off of the temporal interval, always the continuity itself in its modal setting. But when I thus turn back, again and again, to the same beginning point and to the same succession of temporal points, the beginning point itself always sinks steadily ever further back.

§ 21. Levels of Clarity of Reproduction

Thus, what is presentified floats in consciousness in ways more or less clear, and the different modes of lack of clarity refer to the whole which is presentified and to its modes of consciousness. Also with respect to the originary givenness of a

71

temporal Object we find that the Object first appears vividly and clearly and then, with diminishing clarity, goes over into emptiness. These modifications belong to the flux, but while they appear even in the presentification of the flux, still other obscurities confront us, namely, the "clear" (in the first sense) appears as seen through a veil—unclear now and then, that is, more or less unclear, and so forth. Therefore, the two types of lack of clarity are not to be confused. The specific modes of vividness and lack of vividness, of clarity and lack of clarity of the presentification do not belong to what is presentified, or belong to it only by virtue of the modality of the presentification. They belong to the actual lived experience of the presentification.

§ 22. The Certainty of Reproduction

A difference worthy of note also exists with respect to the certainty of primary and secondary remembrance.[13] What I am retentionally aware of, we say, is absolutely certain. What about the more distant past then? If I remember something which I experienced yesterday, then I reproduce the occurrence, if necessary, following all the steps of the succession. While I am doing this, I am conscious of a sequence; one step is first reproduced, then, in definite sequence, the second, and so on. But apart from this sequence, which evidently belongs to the reproduction as the present flow of lived experience, the reproduction brings about the presentation of a temporal flow which is past. And it is entirely possible not only that the individual steps of the occurrence made present through memory deviate from those of the actual past event (that they did not happen as they are now presentified), but also that the real order of succession was other than the order of succession as recollected. It is here, therefore, that errors are possible, errors, that is, which arise from the reproduction as such and are not to be confused with the errors to which

13. Cf. pp. 57ff.

the perception of temporal Objects (namely, of transcendent Objects) is also subject. That this is the case and in what sense this is the case have already been mentioned. If I have been originarily conscious of a temporal succession, it is indubitable that a temporal succession has taken place and takes place. But this is not to say that an (Objective) event really takes place in the sense in which I apprehend it. The individual apprehensions can be wrong, corresponding to no reality. And if the Objective intention of what is apprehended remains in the mode of being shoved back in time [*zeitlichen Zurückgeschobenheit*] (with regard to the constitutive content of what is apprehended and its relation to other objects), the error interpenetrates the entire temporal apprehension of the occurrence which appears. However, if we limit ourselves to the succession of the exhibitive "contents" or of the "appearances" also, an indubitable truth remains: an event has attained givenness, and this succession of appearances has come into existence, even though, perhaps, not the succession of incidents which appears to me.

The question is now whether this certainty of temporal consciousness can be retained in reproduction. This is possible only by means of a coincidence of the reproductive flow with a retentional one. If I have a succession of two notes, C, D, I can, while the memory is still fresh, repeat this succession, in fact, in certain respects, repeat it adequately. I repeat C, D inwardly, being conscious that first C and then D has occurred. And while this consciousness is "still vivid," I can do the same thing again, etc. Undoubtedly, I can in this way go beyond the primordial sphere of certainty. At the same time, we see here the way in which recollection takes place. When I repeat C, D, this reproductive representation of the succession finds its realization in the still vivid earlier succession.[14]

14. One can also take this the other way around, since reproduction makes intuitive the succession of which we are conscious merely in retention.

§ 23. The Coincidence of the Now Reproduced
with a Past Now—The Distinction between
Phantasy and Recollection

After we have contrasted the reproductive consciousness of what is past with the originary, a further problem arises. When I reproduce a melody that I have heard, the phenomenal now of the recollection presentifies something past. In phantasy, in recollection, a tone sounds now. It reproduces the first tone, perchance of the melody which is past. The consciousness of the past given with the second tone reproduces the "just past" that was originarily given earlier, therefore, a past "just past." But how does the reproduced now come to represent something past? A reproduced now certainly places a now immediately before us. Whence comes then the reference to something past, which can still be given originarily only in the form of the "just past"?

To answer this question it is necessary to undertake an analysis which, up to now, we have only touched upon, namely, that regarding the difference between the mere phantasy of a temporally extended Object and recollection. In mere phantasy there is no positing of the reproduced now and no coincidence of this now with one given in the past. Recollection, on the other hand, posits what is reproduced and gives it a position with regard to the actual now and the sphere of the originary temporal field to which the recollection itself belongs.[15] Only in the originary consciousness of time can the connection between a reproduced now and a past be effected. The flux of presentification is a flux of phases of lived experiences constructed exactly like every other temporally constitutive flux and, therefore, is itself temporally constitutive. All the shadings and modifications which constitute the form of time are found here and just as the immanent sound is con-

15. Cf. Appendix III: The Correlational Intentions of Memory and Perception—The Modes of Time-Consciousness, pp. 137ff.

stituted in the flux of tonal phases, so the unity of the presentification of the sound is constituted in the flux of the presentification of the tonal phases. It is certainly generally true that in phenomenological reflection all appearances, imaginings, thoughts, etc., in the broadest sense, lead us back to a flux of constitutive phases which undergo an immanent Objectivation, even the memories, expectations, wishes, etc., belonging to appearances of perception (external perceptions) as unities of internal consciousness. Therefore, presentifications of every kind such as the flow of lived experiences of the universal, temporally constitutive form also constitute an immanent Object: the "enduring, thus and thus flowing process of presentification."

On the other hand, presentifications have the unique property that in themselves and according to all phases of lived experience they are presentifications in another sense, namely, that they have a second intentionality of another sort, one peculiar to them and not characteristic of all lived experiences. This new intentionality has the peculiarity that, as regards its form, it is a counter-image [*Gegenbild*] of the temporally constitutive intentionality, and, like this intentionality, reproduces in every element a moment of a flux of the present, and in totality a total flux of the present. Thus it sets up a reproductive consciousness of a presentified immanent Object. This new intentionality constitutes, therefore, something twofold. First, through its form of the flux of lived experience, it constitutes presentification as immanent unity, and does so in such a way that the moments of the lived experience of this flux are reproductive modifications of the moments of a parallel flux (which in the usual case consists of non-reproductive moments). Second, it constitutes presentification in another way, such that these reproductive modifications signify an intentionality; the flux is knit together into a constitutive whole in which we are conscious of an intentional unity, the unity of the remembered.

§ 24. Protentions in Recollection

In order now to understand the disposition of this constituted unity of lived experience, "memory," in the undivided stream of lived experience, the following must be taken into account: every act of memory contains intentions of expectation whose fulfillment leads to the present. Every primordially constitutive process is animated by protentions which voidly [leer] constitute and intercept [auffangen] what is coming, as such, in order to bring it to fulfillment. However, the recollective process not only renews these protentions in a manner appropriate to memory. These protentions were not only present as intercepting, they have also intercepted. They have been fulfilled, and we are aware of them in recollection. Fulfillment in recollective consciousness is re-fulfillment [Wieder-Erfüllung] (precisely in the modification of the positing of memory), and if the primordial protention of the perception of the event was undetermined and the question of being-other or not-being was left open, then in the recollection we have a pre-directed expectation which does not leave all that open. It is then in the form of an "incomplete" recollection whose structure is other than that of the undetermined, primordial protention. And yet this is also included in the recollection. There are difficulties here, therefore, with regard to the intentional analysis both for the event considered individually, and, in a different way, for the analysis of expectations which concern the succession of events up to the actual present. Recollection is not expectation; its horizon, which is a posited one, is, however, oriented on the future, that is, the future of the recollected. As the recollective process advances, this horizon is continually opened up anew and becomes richer and more vivid. In view of this, the horizon is filled with recollected events which are always new. Events which formerly were only foreshadowed are now quasi-present, seemingly in the mode of the embodied present.

§ 25. The Double Intentionality of Recollection

If, in the case of a temporal Object, we distinguish the content together with its duration (which in connection with "the" time can have a different place) from its temporal position, we have in the reproduction of an enduring being, and in addition to the reproduction of the filled duration, the intentions which affect the position, in fact, necessarily affect it. A duration is not imaginable, or better, is not positable unless it is posited in a temporal nexus, unless the intentions of the temporal nexus are there. Hence it is necessary that these intentions take the form of either past or future intentions. To the duality of the intentions which are oriented on the fulfilled duration and on its temporal position corresponds a dual fulfillment. The entire complex of intuitions which makes up the appearance of past enduring Objects has its possible fulfillment in the system of appearances which belong to the same enduring thing. The intentions of the temporal nexus are fulfilled through the establishment of the fulfilled nexuses up to the actual present. In every presentification, therefore, we must distinguish between the reproduction of the consciousness in which the past enduring Object was given, i.e., perceived or in general primordially constituted, and that consciousness which attaches to this reproduction as constitutive for the consciousness of "past," "present" (coincident with the actual now), and "future."

Now is this last also reproduction? This is a question which can easily lead one astray. Naturally, the whole is reproduced, not only the then present of consciousness with its flux but "implicitly" the whole stream of consciousness up to the living present. This means that as an essential *a priori* phenomenological formation [*Genese*] memory is in a continuous flux because conscious life is in constant flux and is not merely fitted member by member into the chain. Rather, everything new reacts on the old; its forward-moving intention is fulfilled and determined thereby, and this gives the reproduction a definite coloring. An *a priori,* necessary retroaction is thus revealed here. The new points again to the new, which, entering, is determined and modifies the reproductive possibilities for the old, etc. Thereby the retroactive power of the chain goes back, for the past as reproduced bears the character of the past and an indeterminate intention toward a certain state of affairs in regard to the now. It is not true, therefore, that we have a mere chain of "associated" intentions, one after the other, this one suggesting the next (in the stream). Rather, we have an intention which in itself is an intention toward the series of possible fulfillments.

But this intention is a non-intuitive, an "empty" intention, and its objectivity is the Objective temporal series of events, this series being the dim surroundings of what is actually recollected. Can we not characterize the non-general "surroundings" as a unitary intention which is based on a multiplicity of interconnected objectivities and in which a discrete and manifold givenness comes gradually to fulfillment? Such is also the case with the spatial background. And so also, everything in perception has its reverse side as background (for it is not a question of the background of attention but of apprehension). The component "unauthentic perception" which belongs to every transcendent perception as an essential element is a "complex" intention which can be fulfilled in nexuses of a definite kind, in nexuses of data.

The foreground is nothing without the background; the appearing side is nothing without the non-appearing. It is the same with regard to the unity of time-consciousness—the duration reproduced is the foreground; the classifying intentions make us aware of a background, a temporal background. And in certain ways, this is continued in the constitution of the temporality of the enduring thing itself with its now, before, and after. We have the following analogies: for the spatial thing, the ordering into the surrounding space and the spatial world on the one side, and on the other, the spatial thing itself with its foreground and background. For the temporal thing, we have the ordering into the temporal form and the temporal world on the one side, and on the other the temporal thing itself and its changing orientation with regard to the living now.

§ 26. The Difference between Memory and Expectation

We must further investigate whether memory and expectation equal each other. Intuitive remembrance offers me the vivid reproduction of the expiring duration of an event, and only the intentions which refer back to the before and forward to the living now remain unintuitive.

In the intuitive idea of a future event, I now have intuitively the productive "image" of a process which runs off reproductively. Joined thereto are indeterminate intentions of the future and of the past, i.e., intentions which from the beginning of the process affect the temporal surroundings which terminate in the living now. To that extent, expectational intuition is an inverted memorial intuition, for the now-intentions do not go "before" the process but follow after it. As empty environmental intentions, they lie "in the opposite direction." How do matters stand now with the mode of givenness of the process itself? Does it make any essential difference that in memory the content of the process is determinate? Moreover, the memory can be intuitive but still not very determinate, inasmuch as many intuitive components by no means have real memorial character. With "perfect" memory, to be sure, everything would be clear to the last particular and properly characterized as memory. But, ideally, this is also possible with expectation. In general, expectation lets much remain open, and this remaining-open is again a characteristic of the components concerned. But, in principle, a prophetic consciousness (a consciousness which gives itself out as prophetic) is conceivable, one in which each character of the expectation, of the coming into being, stands before our eyes, as, for example, when we have a precisely determined plan and, intuitively imagining what is planned, accept it lock, stock, and barrel, so to speak, as future reality. Still there will also be many unimportant things in the intuitive anticipation of the future which as makeshifts fill out the concrete image. The latter, however, can in various ways be other than the likeness it offers. It is, from the first, characterized as being open.

The principal differences between memory and expectation, however, are to be found in the manner of fulfillment. Intentions of the past are necessarily fulfilled by the establishment of nexuses of intuitive reproductions. The reproduction of past events permits, with respect to their validity (in internal consciousness) only the confirmation of the uncertainties of memory and their improvement by being transformed in a reproduction in which each and everything in the components is characterized as reproductive. Here we are concerned with such questions as: Have I really seen or perceived this? Have I really had this appearance with exactly this content? All this must at the same time dovetail into a context of similar intuitions up to the now. Another question, to be sure, is the following: Was the appearing thing real? On the other hand, expectation finds its fulfillment in a perception. It pertains to the essence of the expected that it is an about-to-be-perceived. In view of this, it is evident that if what is expected makes its appearance, i.e., becomes something present, the expectational situation itself has gone by. If the future has become the present, then the present has changed to the relatively past. The situation is the same with regard to environmental intentions. They are also fulfilled through the actuality of an impressional living experience.

Notwithstanding these differences, expectational intuition is something primordial and unique exactly as is intuition of the past.

§ 27. Memory as Consciousness of Having-Been-Perceived

What follows is of the greatest significance with regard to the characterization of the positing reproductions which have been analyzed. What pertains to their essence is not the mere reproductive positing of temporal being but a certain relation to internal consciousness. It belongs primarily to the essence of memory that it is consciousness of having-been-perceived. If I intuitively remember an external process, I have a reproductive intuition of it. And it is a positing reproduction. We are necessarily cognizant of this external reproduction, however, by means of an internal reproduction.[16] An external appearing in which the external process is given in a determinate mode of appearance must indeed be reproduced. The external appearance as a lived experience is unity of internal consciousness, and internal reproduction conforms to internal consciousness. However, there are two possibilities for the reproduction of a process. It can be a positing internal reproduction, and, accordingly, the appearance of the process can be posited in the unity of immanent time, or it can also be a positing external reproduction which posits the temporal process concerned in Objective time, but does not posit the appearance itself as a process of internal time, and hence, further, does not posit the temporally constitutive stream in the unity of the common life-stream.

Memory, therefore, is not necessarily memory of an earlier perception. However, since the memory of an earlier process includes the reproduction of appearances in which the process came to be given, there is always the possibility of a memory

16. Cf. Appendix XI, pp. 170ff.

of the earlier perception of the process (in other words, the possibility of a reflection in the memory which brings the earlier perception to a state of givenness). The earlier complex of consciousness is reproduced and what is reproduced has both the character of reproduction and the character of the past.

Let us make these relations clear by means of an example. I remember a lighted theater—this cannot mean that I remember having perceived the theater. Otherwise, this would imply that I remember that I have perceived, that I perceived the theater, and so on. I remember the lighted theater; this means that "in my internal consciousness" I see the lighted theater as having been. In the now, I behold the not-now. Perception constitutes the present. In order that a now as such may stand before me, I must perceive. In order to intuitively represent a now, I must effect a perception "in an image" representatively modified. Not in such a way, however, that I represent the perception; rather, I represent what is perceived, i.e., what appears as being present in the perception. The memory really implies, therefore, a reproduction of the earlier perception, but the memory is not in the true sense a representation of the perception. The perception is not meant and posited in the memory. What is meant and posited in the memory is the object of the perception together with its now, which last, moreover, is posited in relation to the actual now. I remember the lighted theater of yesterday, i.e., I effect a "reproduction" of the perception of the theater. Accordingly, the theater hovers before me in the representation as something actually present. I mean this, but at the same time I apprehend this present as lying back in reference to the actual present of perceptions now extant. Naturally, it is now evident that the perception of the theater was; I have perceived the theater. What is remembered appears as having been present, that is, immediately and intuitively. And it appears in such a way that a present intuitively appears which is at an interval from the present of the actual now. The latter present is constituted in the actual perception. The intuitively appearing present, the intuitive representation of the not-now, is constituted in a counter-image of perception, in a "presentification of the earlier perception" in which the theater comes to be given "as if now." This presentification of the perception of the theater is therefore not to be understood as if it were a re-living of the perception. What I intend in the presentification, rather, is the being-present of the perceived Object.

§ 28. Memory and Figurative Consciousness— Memory as Positing Reproduction

Still to be considered is the kind of presentification in question here. It is not a matter of a representation by means of a similar Object, as in the case of a conscious imitation (a painting, bust, or the like). In contrast to this figurative consciousness, reproductions have the character of self-presentification in the sense of what is past. Present memory is a phenomenon wholly analogous to perception. It has the appearance of the object in common with the corresponding perception. However, in the case of memory the appearance has a modified character, by virtue of which the object stands forth not as present but as having been present.

What is essential to the modes of reproduction termed memory and expectation lies in the disposition of the reproduced appearances in the nexus of being of internal time, of the flowing succession of my lived experiences. Normally, the act of positing is extended also to what is objective in external appearance, but this positing can be suspended; it can be contradicted. Even in this case, memory or expectation still remains, i.e., we do not cease calling something like that memory or expectation even if we denote an earlier perception or one to come as merely "supposed." If, from the first, it is a matter not of the reproduction of transcendent but of immanent Objects, then the stages of the formation of reproductive intuitions described drop out, and the positing of what is reproduced coincides with its disposition in the series of lived experiences in immanent time.

§ 29. Memory of the Present

With regard to the sphere of the intuition of external time and objectivity there is yet another type of immediate reproductive intuition of temporal objects to be considered. (Indeed, all our explanations are restricted to the immediate intuition of temporal objects, and the question of mediate or non-intuitive expectations and memories is left alone.)

Whether on the basis of earlier perceptions or on the basis of a description, etc., I can also represent to myself something present as now existing without having it now embodied before me. In the first case, I certainly have a memory, but to what is remembered I grant duration up to the actual now, and for this duration I have no internal, remembered "appearances." The "memory-image" serves me, but I do not posit what is remembered as such, what is objective in the internal memory, in the duration proper to it. What is posited is the enduring as the self-exhibiting in this appearance. We posit the appearing now aₙd the ever-fresh now, etc., but we do not posit it as "past."

We know that the "past" in the case of memory also does not imply that in the present act of remembrance we form an image of the earlier one and others of like construction. Rather, we simply posit the appearing, the intuited, which in conformity with its temporality is naturally intuitable only in modes of temporality. And to what appears thereby we give, in the mode of remembrance and by means of environmental intentions, position with regard to the now of actuality. Therefore, with the presentification of an absent present thing [abwesenden Gegenwärtigen] we must also inquire about the environmental intentions of the intuition, and these are here naturally of a wholly different kind. They have no reference at all to the actual now through a continuous series of internal appearances which were posited jointly. To be sure, this reproductive memory is not without correlation. It is supposed to be an enduring thing which there appears, which has been, now is, and will be. Somehow or other, therefore, I can go there and see, still find the thing, and can then go back again and in repeated "possible" trains of memory establish the intuition. And if I had set out just before and had gone there (and this is an indicated possibility with which possible memory-trains accord) then I should now have this intuition as a perceptual intuition, etc. Therefore the appearance which hovers before me reproductively is certainly not characterized as having been internally impressional. What appears is not characterized as having been perceived in its temporal duration, although a reference to the *hic et nunc* also exists here. The appearance also bears a certain positing character; it belongs in a determinate nexus of appearances (that is, of appearances which are "positing," position-taking, through and through), and in reference to those it has a motivating character. The environmental intention always produces for the "possible" appearances themselves a halo of intentions. Such also is the case with the intuition of enduring being. I now perceive this being and posit it as having been before without having perceived it before and remembering it now. In addition, I posit it as continuing to be in the future.

§ 30. The Preservation of the Objective [gegenständlichen] Intention in the Retentional Modification

It often happens that while the retention of something just past is still vivid, a reproductive image of it appears—naturally, an image of the thing as it was given in the now-point.

We recapitulate, so to speak, what has just been lived and experienced. This internal renewal in presentification sets the reproductive now in relation with the now still living in recent memory. In this way, the consciousness of identity which sets forth the identity of the one or the other comes about. (At the same time, this phenomenon shows that, in addition to the intuitive, a void part which extends very much further belongs in the sphere of primary remembrance. While we still retain something that has been [*ein Gewesenes*], in the fresh, although empty, memory an "image" of this thing can also emerge.) It is a universal and basically essential fact that every now as it sinks into the past maintains its strict identity. Phenomenologically speaking, the now-consciousness that is constituted on the basis of a content A changes continuously to a consciousness of the past, while at the same time an ever new now-consciousness is built up. With this transformation (and this is part of the essence of time-consciousness) the self-modifying consciousness preserves its objective intention.

The continuous modification which every primordial temporal field includes with respect to the character of the act which constitutes it is not to be understood as if, in the series of apprehensions belonging to an Object-phase, a continuous modification took place in the objective intention beginning from the appearance of the apprehensions as now-positing and descending even to the last accessible phenomenal moment of the past. On the contrary, the objective intention remains absolutely the same and identical. Nevertheless, a self-gradating exists and, in fact, not merely with respect to the content of apprehension, which has its diminution, a certain falling off from the greatest peak of sensation in the now to the point of imperceptibility. Above all, the now-moment is characterized as the new. The now, just sinking away, is no longer the new, but that which is shoved aside by the new. In this being-shoved-aside lies an alteration. But while the now which has been shoved aside has lost its now-character, it maintains itself in its objective intention absolutely unaltered. It is intention toward an individual Objectivity, specifically, an intuiting intention. In this respect, therefore, there is no alteration whatsoever. However, it would be wise to consider here what "the preservation of the objective intention" means. The complete apprehension of an object contains two components: the one constitutes the Object according to its extra-temporal determinations; the other creates the temporal position: being-now, having-been, and so on. The Object as temporal matter [*Zeitmaterie*], as that which has temporal position and temporal extensity, as that which endures or is altered, as that which now is and then has been, springs solely from the Objectivation of the contents of apprehension—in the case of sensible Objects, therefore, from the sensible contents. Nevertheless, we must not lose sight of the fact that these contents are temporal Objects, that they are generated in a succession as a continuum of primal impressions and retentions, and that these temporal shadings of the data of sensation have their significance for the temporal determinations of the Objects constituted by means of them. However, their temporal character is of no importance with regard to their nature as representatives of material qualities according to their quiddity [*Was*]. The non-temporally grasped data of apprehension constitute the Object according to its specific state, and where this is preserved we can certainly speak of an identity. However, if heretofore we spoke of the preservation of the objective reference, this implies that the object is maintained not only in its specific state but also as individual, therefore as something temporally determined which sinks back with its temporal determination in time. This sinking back is a peculiar phenomenological modification of the consciousness whereby in relation to the ever newly constituted actual now an ever increasing interval is built up by means of the continuous series of alterations leading to that end.

87

§ 31. Primal Impressions and Objective [objektiver] Individual Temporal Points

Seemingly, we have been led here to an antinomy. The Object, in sinking back, constantly alters its temporal position, and yet in sinking back is said to preserve its temporal position. In truth, however, the Object of primary remembrance constantly being shoved back does not alter its temporal position but only its interval from the actual now, specifically, because the actual now is accepted as an ever new Objective temporal point, whereas the past temporal thing remains what it is. But the question now is, how does it happen that, despite the phenomenon of the continuous alteration of the consciousness of time, there is the consciousness of Objective time, and above all the consciousness of identical temporal positions? Very closely bound to this is the question of the constitution of the Objectivity of individual temporal objects and processes. All Objectification takes place in time-consciousness, and without a clarification of the identity of temporal position no clarification of the identity of an Object in time can be given.

Stated more precisely, the problem is the following: The now-phases of perception constantly undergo a modification. They are not preserved simply as they are. They flow. Constituted therein is what we have referred to as sinking back in time. The tone sounds now and immediately sinks into the past, as the same tone. This affects the tone in each of its phases and, therefore, the whole tone also. Now, through our previous observations, this sinking away is, in some measure, comprehensible. But how is it that despite the sinking away of the tone, we still say, as our analysis of reproductive consciousness has shown, that it has a fixed position in time, that temporal points and temporal positions may be identified in repeated acts? The tone, as well as every temporal point in the unity of the enduring tone, indeed has its absolutely fixed place in "Objective" (or even in immanent) time. Time is motionless and yet it flows. In the flow of time, in the continuous sinking away into the past, there is constituted a non-flowing, absolutely fixed, identical Objective time. This is the problem.

Let us first consider somewhat more closely the state of affairs with regard to the sinking away of the same tone. Why do we say it is the same tone which sinks away? The tone is built up in a temporal flux through its phases. Of every phase, that of an actual now, for example, we know that although subject to the law of constant modification, it still must appear as objectively the same, as the same tonal point, so to speak. This is true because a continuity of apprehension is present here which is governed by the identity of sense and exists in continuous coincidence. This coincidence concerns the extra-temporal matter which even in flux preserves the identity of the objective sense. This holds true for every now-phase. But every new now is precisely that, a new one, and is phenomenologically characterized as such. Even if every tone continues completely unaltered, in such a way that not the least alteration is visible to us—even if every new now, therefore, possesses exactly the same content of apprehension as regards moments of quality, intensity, and the like, and carries exactly the same apprehension—nevertheless, a primordial difference still exists, one which pertains to a new dimension. And this difference is a constant one. From the point of view of phenomenology, only the now-point is characterized as an actual now, that is, as new. The previous temporal point has undergone its modification, the one before that a continuing modification, etc. This continuum of modifications in the content of apprehension and the apprehensions based thereon produce the consciousness of the extension of the tone with the continuous sinking down into the past of what is already extended.

But despite the phenomenon of the continuous alteration

of time-consciousness, how does the consciousness of Objective time and, above all, of identical temporal place and temporal extension come about? The answer is that in contrast to the flux resulting from being shoved back in time, i.e., the flux of modifications of consciousness, the Object which appears to be shoved back remains preserved even in absolute identity, that is, the Object together with the positing as a "this" experienced in the now-point. The continuous modification of apprehension in the constant flux does not affect the "as what" of the apprehension, i.e., the sense. It intends no new Object or Object-phase; it yields no new temporal point, but always the same Object with the same temporal points. Every actual now creates a new temporal point because it creates a new Object, or rather a new Object-point which is held fast in the flux of modifications as one and the same individual Object-point. And the constancy in which again and again a new now is constituted shows us that in general it is not a question of "novelty" but of a constant moment of individuation, in which the temporal position has its origin. It is part of the essence of the modifying flux that this temporal position stands forth as identical and necessarily identical. The now as the actual now is the givenness of the actual present of the temporal position. As a phenomenon moves into the past, the now acquires the character of a past now. It remains the same now, however. Only in relation to the momentarily actual and temporally new now does it stand forth as past.

The Objectivation of temporal Objects rests, therefore, on the following moments. The content of sensation which belongs to the different actual now-points of the Objects can qualitatively remain absolutely unaltered, but even with so far-reaching an identity with regard to content it still does not have true identity. The same sensation now and in another now has a difference, in fact, a phenomenological difference which corresponds to the absolute temporal position. This difference is the primal source of the individuality of the "this" and therewith of the absolute temporal position. Every phase of the modification has "in essence" the same qualitative content and the same temporal moment, although modified. Furthermore, each phase has in itself the same temporal moment in such a way that precisely by means of it the subsequent apprehension of identity is made possible: this on the side of sensation, or of the foundation of apprehension. The different moments sustain different parts of the apprehension, of the true Objectivation. One aspect of the Objectivation finds its support purely in the qualitative content of the material of sensation. This yields the temporal matter, e.g., the sound. This matter is held identically in the flux of the modification of the past. A second aspect of the Objectivation arises from the apprehension of the representatives of the temporal positions [*Zeitstellenrepräsentanten*]. This apprehension is also continuously retained in the flux of modification.

To recapitulate: the tonal point in its absolute individuality is retained in its matter and temporal position, the latter first constituting individuality. To this must be added, finally, apprehension which belongs essentially to the modification and which, while retaining the extended objectivity with its immanent absolute time, allows the continuous shoving-back into the past to appear. In our example of the sound, therefore, each temporal point of the ever fresh sounding and dying away has its material of sensation and its Objectifying apprehension. The sound stands forth as the sound, e.g., of a violin string that is bowed. If we again disregard the Objectifying apprehension and consider only the material of sensation, then, according to its matter, it is always precisely the same note C with its tonal quality and timbre unaltered, its intensity fluctuating, perhaps, and so on. This content, purely as the content of sensation, as it underlies the Objectifying apprehension, is extended, that is, every now has its content, even though materially it may be exactly the same. Absolutely the same C now and later is alike, according to experience, but individually it is other.

The term "individual" here refers to the primordial temporal form of sensation, or, as I can also say, to the temporal form of primordial sensation, here the sensation of the actual now-point and only this. Essentially, however, the now-point itself is to be defined through primordial sensation so that the expressed proposition has to be accepted only as an indication of what is meant. An impression, in contrast to a phantasm, is distinguished by the character of originarity.[17] Now, within the sphere of impressions we must lay stress on primal impressions, which, over against the continuum of modifications, are present in the consciousness of primary remembrance. Primal impressions are absolutely unmodified, the primal source of all further consciousness and being. Primal impressions have for content what is signified by the word *now,* insofar as it is taken in the strictest sense; every new now is the content of a new primal impression. Constantly, a new and ever new impression flares up with ever new matter, now the same, now changing. What separates primal impression from primal impression is the individualizing moment of the primordial impression of temporal positions, which moment is basically different from the moment of quality and the other moments of the content of sensation. The moment of primordial temporal position naturally is nothing for itself. Individuation is nothing in addition to what has individuation. The entire now-point, the whole originary impression, undergoes the modification of the past, and through the latter we have first exhausted the complete concept of the now so far as it is a relative one and points to a "past," as "past" points to the "now." In addition, this modification, to begin with, affects the sensation without nullifying its universal, impressional character. It modifies the total content of the primal impres-

17. Concerning impressions and phantasms, cf. Appendix II, pp. 133ff.

sion both in its matter and its temporal position. It modifies in exactly the sense that a modification of phantasy does, namely, modifying through and through and yet not altering the intentional essence (the total content).

Therefore, the matter is the same matter, the temporal position the same temporal position; only the mode of givenness has been changed. It is givenness of the past. On this material of sensation is erected the entire Objectifying apperception. Even if we merely glance at the content of sensation (disregarding transcendent apperceptions which sometimes are founded thereon) we effect a perception: the "temporal flux." Duration is then before us as a mode of objectivity. Objectivity [*Gegenständlichkeit*] presupposes consciousness of unity, consciousness of identity. Here we grasp the content of every primal sensation as individual [*Selbst*]. This sensation gives an individual tonal point, and this individual point is identically the same in the flux of the modification of the past. The apperception relative to this point remains, in the modification of the past, in constant coincidence, and the identity of this individual is *eo ipso* identity of the temporal position. The continuous springing forth of ever new primal impressions ever and again produces, in the apprehension of these impressions as individual points, new and distinct temporal positions. This continuity produces a continuity of temporal positions. In the flux of modifications of the past, therefore, a continuous, tone-filled segment of time [*Zeitstück*] is present, but in such a way that only a point of this segment is given by means of the primal impression, and from that point on, temporal positions continuously appear in a modified gradation going back into the past.

Every perceived time is perceived as a past which terminates in the present, the present being a boundary-point. Every apprehension, no matter how transcendent it otherwise may be, is bound to this regularity. If we perceive a flight of birds, a squadron of cavalry at a gallop, and the like, we find the de-

93

scribed distinctions in the underlying basis of sensation—ever new primal sensations, their temporal character, which provides their individuation, being carried with them; and on the other side, we find the same modes in the apprehension. Precisely by this means, the Objective itself appears, the flight of birds as primal givenness in the now-point, as complete givenness, though in a continuum of the past which terminates in the now, while the continuously preceding in the continuum of the past is moved ever further back. The appearing event always has the identical, absolute temporal value. Since, following the segment of time that has expired, the event is shoved ever further back into the past, it is shoved back with its absolute temporal position and hence with its entire temporal interval into the past, i.e., the same event with the same absolute temporal extensity continually appears (as long as it appears at all) as identically the same. Only the form of its givenness is different. On the other hand, in the living source-point of the now there also wells up ever fresh primal being, in relation to which the distance from the actual now of the temporal points belonging to the event is constantly increased. Accordingly, the appearance of sinking back, of withdrawing, arises.

§ 32. The Part of Reproduction in the Constitution of the One Objective [objektiven] Time

With the preservation of the individuality of the temporal points in their sinking back into the past, we still do not have, however, consciousness of a unitary, homogeneous, Objective time. In the occurrence of this consciousness, reproductive memory (in its intuitive capacity, as in the form of empty intentions) plays an important role. Every temporal point which has been shoved back can, by means of reproductive memory, be made the null-point of an intuition of time and be repeated. The earlier temporal field, in which what is presently shoved back was a now, is reproduced, and the reproduced now is identified with the temporal point still vivid in recent memory. The individual intention is the same.[18] The temporal field that is reproduced extends further than that actually present. If we take a point of the past in this temporal field, the reproduction, by being shoved along with the temporal field in which this point was the now, provides a further regress into the past, and so on. Theoretically, this process is to be thought of as capable of being continued without limit, although in practice actual memory soon breaks down. It is evident that every temporal point has its before and after, and that the points and intervals coming before cannot be compressed in the manner of an approximation to a mathematical limit, as, let us say, the limit of intensity. If there were such a boundary-point, there would correspond to it a now which nothing preceded, and this is obviously impossible.[19] A now is always and essentially the edge-point [*Randpunkt*] of an interval of time. And it is evident that this entire interval must sink back and thereby its entire magnitude, its entire individuality, is preserved. To be sure, phantasy and reproduction do not make possible an extension of the intuition of time in the sense that the extent of the real, given temporal gradations in simultaneous consciousness is increased. With reference to this, one may perhaps ask: How, with this successive stringing together of temporal fields, does the one Objective time with the one fixed order come to be? The answer proffers the continuous shoving along of the temporal fields, which in truth is no mere temporal stringing together of temporal fields. The segments being shoved along are individually identified in connection with the intuitively continuous regress into the past. If, starting from any actual lived and experienced temporal point—i.e., any one which is originarily given in the temporal

18. Cf. Appendix IV: Recollection and the Constitution of Temporal Objects and Objective Time [*Zeitobjekten und objektiver Zeit*], pp. 143ff.
    19. Cf. pp. 63ff.

field of perception or one which reproduces a distant past—we go back into the past, along, so to speak, a well-established chain of Objectivities which are interconnected and always identified, then the question arises: How is the linear order there established? In such an order every temporal interval, no matter which—even the external continuity with the actual temporal field reproduced—must be a part of a unique chain, continuing to the point of the actual now. Even every arbitrarily phantasied time is subject to the requirement that if one is able to think of it as real time (i.e., as the time of any temporal Object) it must subsist as an interval within the one and unique Objective time.

§ 33. Some A priori Temporal Laws

Obviously, this *a priori* requirement is grounded in the recognition of the immediately comprehensible and fundamental temporal certainties which become evident on the basis of intuitions of the data of temporal position.

If, to begin with, we compare two primal sensations, or correlatively two primal data, both really appearing in one consciousness as now, then they are distinguished from one another through their matter. They are, however, simultaneous; they have identically the same temporal position; they are both now, and in the same now they necessarily have the same value with regard to temporal position.[20] They have the same form of individuation and both are constituted in impressions which belong to the same impressional level. These data are modified in this identity and always retain it in the modification of the past. A primal datum and a modified datum of like or dissimilar content necessarily have different temporal positions—the same if they arise from the same now-point, different if from different now-points. The actual now is *a* now and constitutes *a* temporal position. No matter how

20. On the construction of simultaneity, cf. § 38, pp. 102ff., and Appendix VII, pp. 155ff.

many Objectivities are constituted separately in the now, they all have the same temporal present and retain their simultaneity in flowing off. That the temporal positions have differences, that these are magnitudes, and the like, can here be seen as evident. Also evident are additional truths such as the law of transitivity, namely, the law that if A is earlier than B then B is later than A. It is part of the *a priori* essence of time that the latter is sometimes identified with a continuity of temporal positions, sometimes with the changing Objectivities which fill it; and that the homogeneity of absolute time is necessarily constituted in the flow of the modifications of the past and in the continual welling-forth of a now, of the creative temporal point, of the source-point of temporal positions in general.

Furthermore, it belongs to the *a priori* essence of the state of affairs that sensation, apprehension, position-taking, all share in the *same* temporal flux and that Objectified absolute time is necessarily the same as the time which belongs to sensation and apprehension. Pre-Objectified time, which pertains to sensation, necessarily founds the unique possibility of an Objectivation of temporal positions which corresponds to the modification of the sensation and the degree of this modification. To the Objectified temporal point in which, let us say, a peal of bells begins, corresponds the temporal point of the matching sensation. In the beginning phase, the sensation has the same time, i.e., if subsequently it is made into an object, it necessarily maintains the temporal position which coincides with the corresponding temporal position of the bell-peal. In the same way, the time of the perception and the time of the perceived are necessarily the same.[21] The act of perception sinks back in time in the same way as the perceived in the appearance, and in reflection each phase of the perception must be given identically the same temporal position as the perceived.

21. Cf. Appendix V: The Simultaneity of Perception and the Perceived, pp. 146ff.

THE LEVELS OF CONSTITUTION OF TIME AND TEM-
PORAL OBJECTS [OBJECTE]

§ 34. The Differentiation of the Levels of Constitution [22]

Proceeding from the most obvious phenomena, after we have studied time-consciousness according to several principal lines of thought and indifferent strata, it would be wise to determine the different levels of constitution in their essential structure and go through them in a systematic way.

We discovered:

1. The things of experience in Objective time (whereby still different levels of empirical being were to be differentiated which hitherto had not been taken into account: the experiential thing of the individual subject, the intersubjectively identical thing, the thing of physics).

2. The constitutive multiplicities of appearances of different levels, the immanent unities in pre-empirical time.

3. The absolute, temporally constitutive flux of consciousness.

§ 35. Differences between the Constituted Unities and the Constitutive Flux [23]

This absolute consciousness which precedes all constitution must first of all be discussed somewhat more closely. Its unique quality stands out clearly in contrast to the constituted unities of the most diverse levels.

1. Every individual Object (every Object in the stream of constituted unity, be it immanent or transcendental) endures,

22. Compare to this and the following sections Appendix VI: Comprehension of the Absolute Flux—Perception in the Fourfold Sense, pp. 149ff.
23. Cf. pp. 152ff.

and necessarily endures, i.e., it is continuous in time and is identical in this continuous being, which also can be considered as process. Conversely, what is in time is continuous in time and is unity of the process, which inseparably carries with it unity of what endures in the procedure. In the tonal process lies the unity of the tone which endures during the process and, conversely, the unity of the tone is unity in the fulfilled duration, i.e., in the process. Therefore, if anything whatsoever is determined as existing in a temporal point, it is thinkable only as the phase of a process in which the duration of an individual being also has its point.

2. In principle, individual or concrete being is invariant or variant; the process is a process of alteration or is static. The enduring Object itself is altering or static. Every alteration, therefore, has its rate of alteration or "acceleration" (metaphorically speaking) with reference to the same duration. In principle, every phase of alteration can broaden into something static, every phase of the static can lead to an alteration.

If, in comparison therewith, we now consider the constitutive phenomena, we find a flux, and every phase of this flux is a continuity of shading. However, in principle, no phase of this flux is to be broadened out to a continuous succession; therefore, the flux should not be thought to be so transformed that this phase is extended in identity with itself. Quite to the contrary, we find necessarily and essentially a flux of continuous "alteration," and this alteration has the absurd property [das Absurde] that it flows exactly as it flows and can flow neither "more swiftly" nor "more slowly." Consequently, any Object which is altered is lacking here, and inasmuch as in every process "something" proceeds, it is not a question here of a process. There is nothing here which is altered, and therefore it makes no sense to speak here of something that endures. It is also senseless, therefore, to wish to find anything which in a duration is not once altered.

§ 36. The Temporally Constitutive Flux as Absolute Subjectivity

It is evident, then, that temporally constitutive phenomena are, in principle, objectivities other than those constituted in time. They are not individual Objects, in other words, not individual processes, and terms which can be predicated of such processes cannot be meaningfully ascribed to them. Therefore, it can also make no sense to say of them (and with the same conceptual meaning) that they are in the now and have been previously, that they succeed one another temporally or are simultaneous with respect to one another, etc. To be sure, one can and must say that a certain continuity of appearance, namely, one which is a phase of the temporally constitutive flux, belongs to a now, namely, to that which it constitutes, and belongs to a before, namely, as that which is (one cannot say was) constitutive of the before. But is not the flux a succession? Does it not, therefore, have a now, an actual phase, and a continuity of pasts of which we are conscious in retentions? We can only say that this flux is something which we name in conformity with what is constituted, but it is nothing temporally "Objective." It is absolute subjectivity and has the absolute properties of something to be denoted metaphorically as "flux," as a point of actuality, primal source-point, that from which springs the "now," and so on. In the lived experience of actuality, we have the primal source-point and a continuity of moments of reverberation [*Nachhallmomenten*]. For all this, names are lacking.

§ 37. Appearances of Transcendent Objects [Objekte] as Constituted Unities

It is further to be noted that when we speak of the "act of perception" and say that it is the point of authentic perceiving to which a continuous sequence of retentions is joined, we have described thereby no immanent temporal unities but precisely moments of the flux. That is, the appearance, let us say, of a house is a temporal being which endures, is altered, etc. This is also the case with the immanent sound which is not an appearance. But the appearance of a house is not the perceptional consciousness and the retentional consciousness [of the house]. These can be understood only as temporally constitutive, as moments of the flux. In precisely the same way, memorial appearance (or the remembered immanent [Immanent], perhaps the remembered immanent primary content) is to be distinguished from memorial consciousness with its retentions of memory. We must distinguish at all times: consciousness (flux), appearance (immanent Object), and transcendent object (if it is not the primary content of an immanent Object). Not all consciousness has reference to the Objectively (i.e., transcendently) temporal, to Objective individuality, as, e.g., that of external perception. In every consciousness we find an "immanent content;" with the content we call "appearance" this is either appearance of the individual (of an external temporal thing) or appearance of the non-temporal. In the act of judgment, for example, I have the appearance "judgment," namely, as immanent temporal unity, and therein "appears" the judgment in the logical sense.[24] The act of judgment always has the character of the flux. At all times, then, that which in *Logischen Untersuchungen* is termed an "act" or an "intentional lived experience" is a flux in which an immanent temporal unity (a judgment, wish, etc.) is constituted. Such a unity has its immanent duration and perhaps proceeds more or less rapidly. These unities which are constituted in the absolute stream are in immanent time, which is *one,* and in this time there is a simultaneous element [*ein Gleichzeitig*] and duration of the same length (or possibly the same duration, that is, for two immanent, simultaneously enduring Objects), also a certain determinability according to before and after.

24. "Appearance" is used here in the wider sense.

§ 38. Unity of the Flux of Consciousness and the Constitution of Simultaneity and Succession [25]

We have already occupied ourselves with the constitution of such immanent Objects and their growth from ever new primal sensations and modifications.[26] In reflection, however, we find a single stream which breaks down into many streams. This plurality, though, still has a unitariness [*Einheitlichkeit*] which talk of a flux both admits and requires. We find many streams, inasmuch as many series of primal impressions begin and end. However, we also find a connecting form, inasmuch as, for all, not merely does the law of the transformation of the now into the no longer and, on the other side, of the not yet into the now function separately, but also something akin to a common form of the now exists, a likeness generally in the mode of the flux. Several, a great many, primal impressions are "all at once," and if any one passes away, the plurality passes "at the same time" and in a completely similar way, with completely similar gradations, and in completely the same tempo. The only difference is that the one stops altogether, while the plurality still has its not-yet, i.e., its fresh primal impressions before itself, which impressions still carry on the duration of what is known through them. Or more clearly: the many primal sensations flow and from the first have at their disposal the same modes of running-off. Only the series of primal impressions which are constitutive for immanent enduring Objects is continued in a far different way, corresponding to the different mode of duration of immanent Objects. They do not make use of the formal possibilities all in the same way. Immanent time is constituted as one for all immanent Objects and processes. Correlatively, the consciousness of time of immanent things is single [*eine Alleinheit*]. The "all-together" [*Zusammen*], the "all-at-once" [*Zugleich*], of

25. Cf. Appendix VII, The Constitution of Simultaneity, pp. 155ff.
26. Cf. § 11, pp. 50ff.

the actual primal sensations is all-embracing; also all-embracing is the "before," the "having-gone-before," of all primal sensations which have just gone before, the regular transformation of this "all-together" of primal sensations into such a before. This before is a continuity and each one of its points is a homogeneous, identical form of running-off for the entire all-together. The law that underlies the entire "all-together" of primal sensations states that the all-together is changed into a stable continuum of modes of consciousness, of modes of expiredness [Abgelaufenheit], and that with the same constancy an ever fresh all-together of primal sensations springs forth originarily to again pass continuously over into expiredness. What is an all-together qua all-together of primal sensations remains an all-together in the mode of expiredness. Primal sensations have their continuous "one after the other" in the sense of a continuous running-off, and primal sensations have their all-together, their "all-at-once." Those which are all at once are real primal sensations; in the mode of succession, however, is a sensation or a group of the all-together, a real primal sensation. The others have expired. But what does this mean? Here, one can say nothing further than: "See." A primal sensation or a group of primal sensations of which we are aware in an immanent now (a tonal now, in the same now a color, etc.) is continually changed in modes of the before-consciousness [Vorhinbewusstsein] in which we are aware of the immanent Object as past, and "all at once" together therewith, as ever new primal sensation appears. An ever fresh now is established and we are conscious thereby of an ever fresh configurational now [Gestaltjetzt], tonal now, and so on. In a group of primal sensations, one is distinguished from the other through the content. Only the now is the same. According to its form, consciousness as consciousness of primal sensation is identical.

But "together" with the consciousness of primal sensations are continuous series of modes of passing [Verlaufsmodi] of "earlier" primal sensations, of earlier now-consciousness. This all-together is an all-together of form as regards continuously modified modes of consciousness, while the all-together of primal sensations is an all-together of open modes, identical as to form. In the continuity of modes of running-off we can extract a point; then we shall also find in this point an all-together of modes of running-off which are like in form or, rather, an identical mode of running-off. Both types of all-together must be essentially distinguished from one another. The one is fundamental to the constitution of simultaneity, the other to the constitution of temporal succession; albeit, on the other hand, simultaneity is never without temporal succession and temporal succession never without simultaneity. Consequently, simultaneity and temporal succession must be correlatively and inseparably constituted. Terminologically, we can distinguish between the fluxional before-all-at-once [*Vor-Zugleich*] and the impressional all-at-once of fluxions. But we cannot refer to either the one or the other mode of being all-at-once as a mode of simultaneity. We can no longer speak of a time of the final constitutive consciousness. Primordially constituted with the primal sensations which initiate the retentional process is the simultaneity, let us say, of a color and a sound, their being in an "actual now," but the primal sensations themselves are not simultaneous, and we cannot call the phases of the fluxional before-all-at-once simultaneous phases of consciousness any more than we can call the succession of consciousness a temporal succession.

What this before-at-the-same-time is we know from our earlier analysis; it is a continuum of phases which are joined to a primal sensation, and every retentional consciousness of an earlier now ("primordial remembrance" of it) is of this continuum. In view of this, we must take into consideration that when the primal sensation recedes, being continuously modified, we not only have in general a lived experience which is a modification of the earlier one, but also can have so turned our regard toward it that in the modified one we "see," so to speak, the earlier not-modified one. When a not too rapid succession of sounds runs off we can, after the running-off of the first sound, not only "look at" it as at something "still present" although no longer sensed but also observe that the mode of consciousness which this sound just now has is a "memory" of the mode of consciousness of the primary sensation in which it was given as now. Thereupon, however, a sharp distinction must be made between the consciousness of the past (the retentional and likewise the "re"-presentification) in which we are conscious of an immanent temporal Object as before, and the retention or the recollective "reproduction" (depending on whether it is a question of the primordial flux of the modification of sensation or of its re-presentification of the earlier primal sensation). And so also for every other fluxion.

If any phase of the duration of an immanent Object is a now-phase, therefore, one we are conscious of in a primal sensation, then conjoining retentions are continuously united with this primal sensation in the before-all-at-once. These retentions are characterized in themselves as modifications of primal impressions which belong to all the remaining, expired temporal points of the constituted duration. Each is consciousness of the past of the corresponding earlier now-point and gives this point in the mode of the before corresponding to its position in the expired duration.

§ 39. The Double Intentionality of Retention and the Constitution of the Flux of Consciousness [27]

The duality in the intentionality of retention gives us a clue to the solution of the difficulty of determining how it is possible to have knowledge of a unity of the ultimate consti-

27. Cf. Appendix VIII. The Double Intentionality of the Stream of Consciousness, pp. 157ff.

tutive flux of consciousness. There is no doubt that there is a difficulty here. If a complete flux (one belonging to an enduring process or Object) has expired, I can still look back on it. It forms, so it appears, a unity in memory. Obviously, therefore, the flux of consciousness is also constituted in consciousness as a unity. In this flux, for example, the unity of the duration of the sound is constituted. The flux itself, however, as the unity of the consciousness of the duration of the sound, is again constituted. And must we then also not say further that this unity is constituted in a wholly analogous fashion and is just as good a constituted temporal series and that one must still speak, therefore, of a temporal now, before, and after?

In conformity with the preceding statements, we can give the following answer: It is the one unique flux of consciousness in which the immanent temporal unity of the sound and also the unity of the flux of consciousness itself are constituted. As startling (if not at first sight even contradictory) as it may appear to assert that the flux of consciousness constitutes its own unity, it is still true, nevertheless. And this can be made intelligible through the essential constitution of the flux itself. The regard can on occasion be guided by the phases which "coincide" as intentionalities of sound in the continuous development of the flux. But the regard can also focus on the flow, on a section of the flow, or on the passage of the flowing consciousness from the beginning to the end of the sound. Every shading off of consciousness which is of the "retentional" kind has a double intentionality: one is auxiliary to the constitution of the immanent Object, of the sound. This is what we term "primary remembrance" of the sound just sensed, or more plainly just retention of the sound. The other is that which is constitutive of the unity of this primary remembrance in the flux. That is, retention is at one with this, that it is further-consciousness [Noch-Bewusstsein]; it is that which holds back, in short, it is precisely retention,

retention of the tonal retention which has passed. In its continuous shading-off in the flux, it is continuous retention of the continuously preceding phases. If we keep any phase whatsoever of the flux of consciousness in view (in the phase appears a tonal now and an interval of duration in the mode of just-having-flowed-away [*Soeben-Abgeflossenheit*]), this phase is concerned with a uniform continuity of retentions in the before-all-at-once. This is retention of the entire momentary continuity of continuously preceding phases of the flux. (In the beginning member it is a new primal sensation; in each leading member that now continuously follows, in the first phase of shading-off, it is immediate retention of the preceding primal sensation. In the next momentary phase it is retention of the retention of the preceding primal sensation, and so on.) If we now let the flux flow away, we then have the flux-continuum as running-off, which allows the continuity just described to be retentionally modified, and thereby every new continuity of phases momentarily existing all-at-once is retention with reference to the total continuity of what is all-at-once in the preceding phase. Hence, a longitudinal intentionality [*Längs-intentionalität*] goes through the flux, which in the course of the flux is in continuous unity of coincidence with itself. Flowing in absolute transition, the first primal sensation changes into a retention of itself, this retention into a retention of this retention, and so on. Conjointly with the first retention, however, a new "now," a new primal sensation, is present and is joined continuously but momentarily with the first retention, so that the second phase of the flux is a primal sensation of the new now and a retention of the earlier one. The third phase, again, is a new primal sensation with retention of the second primal sensation and a retention of the retention of the first, and so on. Here we must take into account that retention of a retention has intentionality not only with reference to what is immediately retained but also with reference to what is retained in the retaining of the second level and finally with reference to the primal datum, which here is thoroughly Objectified. Analogous to this is the way in which presentification of the appearance of a thing has intention not only with reference to this appearance but also with reference to the appearing thing itself. A still better analogy can be drawn from the way in which a memory of A not only makes us conscious of the memory but also makes us conscious of A as that which is remembered in the memory.

Accordingly, we believe that these retentions, constituted in the flux of consciousness by means of the continuity of the retentional modifications and conditions, are continuous retentions of the continuously preceding ones; they are the unity of the flux itself as a one-dimensional, quasi-temporal order. If I orient myself on a sound, I enter attentively into "transverse-intentionality" (always experiencing unity in primal sensation as sensation of the actual tonal now, in retentional modifications as primary remembrances of the series of tonal points which have expired and in the flux of retentional modifications of primal sensations and retentions already on hand); then the enduring sound is present there, ever widening in its duration. If I adapt myself to the "longitudinal intentionality" and to what is self-constituting in it, then I turn my reflective regard from the sound (which has endured for such and such a period) to what is new in the primal sensation at a point in the before-all-at-once and to what is retained "conjointly" therewith following a continuous series. What is retained is past consciousness in its series of phases (first of all, its preceding phase). Then, in the constant flowing-forth of consciousness, I grasp the retained series of expired consciousness with the boundary-point of the actual primal sensation and the continuous shoving-back of this series with the fresh onset of retentions and primal sensations.

One can ask here: Can I find and lay hold of at a glance the entire retentional consciousness of the past flow of consciousness, this retentional consciousness being enclosed in a before-all-at-once? Obviously, the necessary process is this: I must first grasp the before-all-at-once, which is retentionally modified; indeed, it is what it is only in flux. Now, the flux, so far as it modifies this before-all-at-once, is intentionally in coincidence with itself. This constitutes unity in the flux and the one and identical element maintains a constant mode of being shoved back. An ever new element is joined on in front only to immerge again immediately in its momentary nexus. During this process, the regard can remain fixed on the momentary all-at-once which sinks down, but the constitution of the retentional unity reaches out beyond this and adds to the ever new. The regard can be directed thereon in the process, and it is always consciousness in flux as constituted unity.

Consequently, like two aspects of one and the same thing, there are in the unique flux of consciousness *two* inseparable, homogeneous *intentionalities* which require one another and are interwoven with one another. By means of the one, immanent time is constituted, i.e., an Objective time, an authentic time in which there is duration and alteration of that which endures. In the other is constituted the quasi-temporal disposition of the phases of the flux, which ever and necessarily has the flowing now-point, the phase of actuality, and the series of pre-actual and post-actual (of the not yet actual) phases. This pre-phenomenal, pre-immanent temporality is constituted intentionally as the form of temporally constitutive consciousness and in the latter itself. The flux of the immanent, temporally constitutive consciousness not only *is,* but is so remarkably and yet so intelligibly constituted that a self-appearance of the flux necessarily subsists in it, and hence the flux itself must necessarily be comprehensible in the flowing. The self-appearance of the flux does not require a second flux, but *qua* phenomenon it is constituted in itself.[28] The constitut-

28. Cf. Appendix IX: Primal Consciousness and the Possibility of Reflection, pp. 161ff.

ing and the constituted coincide, yet naturally they cannot coincide in every respect. The phases of the flux of consciousness in which phases of the same flux of consciousness are phenomenally constituted cannot be identical with these constituted phases, and they are not. What is caused to appear in the momentary-actual [*Momentan Aktuellen*] of the flux of consciousness is the past phase of the flux of consciousness in the series of retentional moments of this flux.

§ 40. The Constituted Immanent Content

Let us now go over to the level of the immanent "content," whose constitution is the work of the absolute flux of consciousness, and consider it somewhat more closely. This immanent content is made up of lived experiences in the usual sense: the data of sensation (even if unnoticed), for example, a red, a blue, and the like; further, appearances (the appearance of a house, of the environment, etc.), whether or not we pay attention to them and their "objects." In addition, there are the "acts" of asserting, wishing, willing, and so on, and the reproductive modifications (phantasies, memories) pertaining to them. All are contents of consciousness, contents of primal consciousness which is constitutive of temporal objects. Primal consciousness, it should be noted, is not in this sense again a content, an object in phenomenological time.

The immanent contents are what they are only so far as during their "actual" duration they refer ahead to something futural and back to something past. In this reference thither and back, however, there is still something different to be distinguished. In each primal phase which primordially constitutes the immanent content we have retentions of the preceding and protentions of the coming phases of precisely this content, and these protentions are fulfilled as long as this content endures. These "determinate" retentions and protentions have an obscure horizon. Flowing, they pass over into indeterminate ones with reference to the past and future running-off of the stream. Through these retentions and protentions, the actual content of the stream is joined together. From retentions and protentions, then, we must distinguish those recollections and expectations which are not directed toward the constitutive phases of the immanent content but which presentify past or future immanent contents. The contents endure: they have their time; they are individual Objectivities which are the unities of alteration or constancy [*Unveränderung*].

§ 41. Self-Evidence of the Immanent Content— Alteration and Constancy

If one speaks of the self-evident givenness of an immanent content, it is obvious that this self-evidence cannot mean indubitable certainty with regard to the temporal existence of a sound at a point. Self-evidence so grasped (as, is admitted by Brentano, for example) I would hold to be a fiction. If to be extended in time belongs to the essence of a content given in perception, then the indubitableness of the perception can mean nothing other than indubitableness with reference to the temporally extended existent.[29] And this signifies again that any question directed toward individual existence can find its answer only by means of a regress to perception which gives us individual existence in the strictest sense. To the extent that perception itself is yet mixed with what is not perception, to this extent perception itself is still doubtful. However, if it is a matter of immanent content and not of empirical materialities, then duration and alteration, coexistence and succession are completely and entirely to be realized in perceptions, and often enough are actually realized. It happens that in perceptions those which are purely intuitive are perceptions which in the true sense are constitutive of the enduring or changing

29. Concerning internal perception, cf. § 44, pp. 122ff.

contents as such. These are perceptions which in themselves contain nothing further that is questionable. We are led back to these perceptions in all questions regarding origins, but they themselves exclude any further question as to origin. It is clear that the much-talked-of certainty of internal perception, the evidence of the *cogito,* would lose all meaning and significance if we excluded temporal extension from the sphere of self-evidence and true givenness.

Let us now consider the self-evident consciousness of duration and analyze this consciousness itself. If the note C is perceived (and not merely the quality C, but the entire tonal content, which must remain absolutely unaltered) and given as enduring, then the note C is extended over an interval of the immediate temporal field, i.e., another note does not appear in each now but always and continually the same note. That the same note always appears, that there is this continuity of identity, is an internal characteristic of consciousness. The temporal positions are not separated from one another through divisive acts. The unity of perception is here a breachless unity which dispenses with all interrupting internal differences. On the other hand, differences do exist so far as every temporal point is distinct from every other—only distinct, however, not separated. The indistinguishable likeness of temporal matter and the constancy of the modification of the time-positing consciousness essentially establish the coalescence into unity of the breachless extension, and therewith a concrete unity first comes into being. Only as temporally extended is the note C a concrete individual. The concrete is, at any time, the only given, and obviously included under the concrete are intellective processes of analysis which make possible explications such as the one just attempted. The breachless unity of the note C, which is the primary given, proves to be a divisible unity, a coalescence of moments ideally to be distinguishable therein and, if the occasion should arise, to be found therein—for example, by means of simultaneous succession by which sections in the duration running off parallel are distinguishable, and with reference to which a comparison and identification can then take place.

For the rest, we operate with descriptions which already are in some respects idealizing fictions. It is a fiction, for example, that a sound endures completely unaltered. In any moment, no matter what, a greater or lesser fluctuation will always take place, and thus the continuous unity with respect to a given moment will be linked to a difference of another moment which provides an indirect separation from the first. The breach of qualitative identity, the spring from one quality to another within the same genus of quality in a temporal position, yields a new lived experience, the lived experience of change, whereby it is evident that a discontinuity is not possible in every temporal point of a temporal interval. Discontinuity presupposes continuity, be it in the form of changeless duration or of continuous alteration. As regards the latter, the continuous alteration, the phases of the consciousness of change also go over into one another without a break, therefore, in the mode of the unity of the consciousness of identity, just as in the case of changeless duration. But the unity does not turn out to be undifferentiated unity. What at first sight goes over, one into the other, without differentiation, exhibits in the development of the continuous synthesis variation and ever greater variation. Thus similarity and difference are mingled and a continuity of increase of the difference is given with increasing extension. Because it is individually preserved, the primordial now-intention appears in the ever new simultaneous consciousness, posited in one with intentions which, the further they stand temporally from the now-intention, the more they throw into relief an ever increasing difference or disparity. What is at first coincident and then nearly coincident becomes ever more widely separated; the old and the new no longer appear to be in essence completely the same but as ever different and strange, despite similarity as to kind.

113

In this way arises the consciousness of the "gradually changed," of the growing disparity in the flux of continuous identification.

In the case of duration without alteration we have a continuous consciousness of unity which in advancing always remains a homogeneous consciousness of unity. The coincidence is posited throughout the entire series of constantly advancing intentions and the pervading unity is always unity of a coincidence. It allows no consciousness of "being other," of deviation or disparity to enter. In the consciousness of alteration we also find coincidence, which in certain ways likewise permeates the entire temporal extension. However, in the coincidence as regards the general there also appears an ever-growing divergence with regard to the difference. The way in which the matter of the alteration is distributed over the temporal interval determines the consciousness of the fast or slow alteration and its rate and acceleration. In every case, however, not merely in that of continuous acceleration, the consciousness of otherness, of difference, presupposes a unity. In change, and likewise with alteration, something enduring must be present—something which makes up the identity of that which is altered or undergoes a change. Obviously, this refers back to the essential forms of consciousness of an individual. If the quality of the sound remains unaltered and the intensity or timbre changes, we say that the *same* sound has changed in timbre or has been altered with respect to intensity. If in the whole phenomenon nothing remains unaltered, if it changes "in every respect," then even in this case there is always still enough to establish unity, namely, the indistinguishableness with which adjoining phases go over into one another and in so doing produce consciousness of unity. The mode and form of the whole remains the same as to kind. The similar passes over into the similar within a manifold of similarity and conversely. The similar is that which can belong to a unity of continuous transition; or everything which has a difference is

114

—as with the like—such that it can establish the unity of a changeless duration (rest), i.e., that which has no difference. So it is, therefore, everywhere whenever we speak of alteration and change. A consciousness of unity underlies it.

§ 42. Impression and Reproduction

At the same time, we should note that if we follow up, not the constitution of impressional contents in their duration, but, let us say, that of the remembered contents, we cannot speak of primal impressions which conform to the now-point of these contents. At the head of things here stand primary remembrances (as absolute phases), not something inserted, primally engendered-originated [*Urgezeugt-Entsprungenes*] "from without" "alien to consciousness;" but we could say (at least with memory) something which emerges or re-emerges. This moment, although itself not an impression, is still, like an impression, not a product of spontaneity but in certain respects something perceptive. One can also speak here of passive reception, and distinguish the passive reception which gathers in the novel, strange, and originary and the passive reception which merely brings back or presentifies.

Every constituted lived experience is either an impression or a reproduction. As reproduction, it is either *re*-presentation [*Ver-gegenwärtigen*] or it is not. In any case it is itself something (immanently) present. But to every present and pre-senting consciousness there corresponds the ideal possibility of an exactly matching presentification of this consciousness. To impressional perception corresponds the possibility of a presentification of it; to impressional desiring corresponds a presentification of it, and so on. This presentification also concerns every sensible content of sensation. To sensed red corresponds a phantasm of red, presentificational consciousness of impressional red. To what is sensed (i.e., to the perception of hyletic data) there corresponds a presentification of the act

115

of sensing. Every act of presentification, however, is itself actually present through an impressional consciousness. In a certain sense, then, all lived experiences are known through impressions or are impressed. Among them, however, are those which occur as presentifying modifications of consciousness, and to every consciousness there corresponds such a modification. (In view of this, therefore, presentification is not at the same time to be understood as an attentive act of meaning.) An act of perception is consciousness of an object. As consciousness, it is also an impression, something immanently present. To this immanent presentation, to the perception of an A, corresponds the reproductive modification, the presentification of the act of perception, the act of perception in phantasy or memory. Such a "perception in phantasy" is at the same time, however, a phantasy of the perceived Object. In perception, an Object, let us say, a thing or concrete process, stands forth as present. The perception, therefore, is not only present itself, it is also a presentation. In it something actually present stands forth—the thing, the process. In just the same way, a presentificational modification of the perception is also a presentification of the perceived Object; the thing-Object [*Dingobjekt*] is phantasied, remembered, expected.

In primordial consciousness are constituted all impressions, primary content such as lived experiences which are "consciousness of." For all lived experiences divide into these two fundamental classes: the one class of lived experiences consists of acts which are "consciousness of." These are lived experiences which have "reference to something." The other lived experiences do not. The sensed color does not have a reference to anything.[30] Neither does the content of phantasy,

---

30. Insofar as one has the right to characterize primal consciousness—the flux which constitutes immanent time and the lived experiences which pertain to it—as being itself an act, or to reduce it to unities and acts, then one can and indeed must say: a primal act or nexus of primal acts constitutes unities which themselves are either acts or not. This, however, leads to difficulties.

e.g., a phantasm of red as a red floating before the mind (although not taken notice of). To be sure, however, phantasy-consciousness *of* red, and, indeed, all primitive presentifications do have such a reference. We find, therefore, impressions which are presentifications of impressional consciousness. As impressional consciousness is consciousness of the immanent, so also impressional presentification is presentification of the immanent.

An impression (in the narrower sense, in contrast to presentification) is to be grasped as primary consciousness which has no further consciousness behind it in which we are aware of it. On the other hand, presentification, including the most primitive immanent presentification, is, as such, secondary consciousness. It presupposes primary consciousness in which we are impressionally aware of it.

§ 43. The Constitution of Thing-Appearances [Dingercheinungen] and Things—Constituted Apprehensions and Primal Apprehensions

Let us consider such a primary consciousness, let us say, the perception of this copper ash tray. It stands forth as enduring, material being. On reflection we can distinguish: (1) the perception itself (the concrete perceptual apprehension taken together with the data of apprehension: the perceptual appearance in the mode of certainty, for example), and (2) the perceived (which is to be described in self-evident judgments based on perception). The perceived is also what is meant; the act of meaning "lives" in the act of perception. The perceptual apprehension in its modes is, as reflection teaches, itself something immanently and temporally constituted, standing forth in the unity of presentness [*Gegenwärtigkeit*] although it is not meant. It is constituted through the multiplicity of now-phases and retentions. The contents of apprehension, as well as the intentions of apprehension to which the mode of certainty belongs, are constituted in this way. The contents of sensation are constituted as unities in sensible impressions, the apprehensions in other act-impressions involved with them. Perception as a constituted phenomenon is, in its turn, perception of the thing.

The thing-appearance is constituted in the primary apprehension of time, the thing-apprehension as an enduring, unaltered phenomenon or as one that is altered. And in the unity of this alteration we are "conscious of" a new unity: the unity of the unaltered or altering thing, unaltered or altering in its time, its duration. In the same impressional consciousness in which the perception is constituted, the perceived is also constituted and in exactly the same way. It belongs to the essence of a consciousness so constructed that it is a consciousness of unity which at the same time is of both a transcendent and an immanent kind. And it also belongs to the essence of this consciousness that an intentional regard can be directed now on the material sensation, now on the appearance, now on the object. The same holds, *mutatis mutandis,* for all "acts." At all times, it belongs to the essence of these acts to have intentionality of a transcendent kind, an intentionality they are able to have only through something immanently constituted, through "apprehensions." And at all times, this establishes the possibility of setting the immanent, the apprehension with its immanent content, in relation to the transcendent. And this setting-in-relation again results in an "act," an act of a higher level.

At the same time, it is well to consider that in perception a complex of contents of sensation, which themselves are constituted unities in the primordial temporal flux, undergoes unity of apprehension. And the unitary apprehension is in its turn a constituted unity in the first sense. We are not conscious of immanent unities in their constitution in the same way that we are conscious of what appears in transcendent appearance or of what is perceived in transcendent perception. On the other hand, they must still have a community of essence. For an immanent impression is an act of presentation just as perception is. In the one case we have an immanent presentation, in the other a transcendent presentation "through" appearances. Therefore, while transcendent appearances are unities constituted in internal consciousness, other unities, namely, the appearing Objects, must again be constituted "in" these unities.

As we saw, the immanent unities are constituted in the flux of multiplicities of temporal shading. We have there, pertaining to every temporal point of the immanent content, following in the flux of consciousness along the longitudinal direction, the diverse, modified contents which are characterized as retentional modifications of the primal content in the now-character. And these primal contents are carriers of primal apprehensions which in their flowing nexus constitute the temporal unity of the immanent content in its moving back into the past. The "contents," in the case of perceptual appearance, are just these complete appearances as temporal unities. Therefore, perceptual apprehension is also constituted in such a multiplicity of shading which becomes homogeneous through the unity of temporal apprehension. We must, therefore, understand apprehension here in a twofold sense: as that which is immanently constituted, and as that which belongs to the immanent constitution, to the phases of the primordial flux itself, the primal apprehension which is no longer constituted. In the immanent flowing-off of appearances, in the continual succession of apprehensions in phenomenological time which we call perception, there is constituted now a temporal unity, insofar as the continuity of apprehensions yields not only unity of the altering appearances (as, for example, the series of aspects provided by the rotation of a thing which appear as aspects of the same thing) but also the unity of the appearances of an enduring or altering thing.

Immanent time is Objectified to a time of Objects constituted in immanent appearances by this means: that in the multiplicity of shading of the contents of sensation as unities of phenomenological time—in other words, in the phenomenological-temporal multiplicity of shading of apprehensions of these contents—appears an identical materiality [*Dinglichkeit*] which continually manifests itself in all phases in multiplicities of shading.[31] The thing is constituted in the flowing-off of its appearances, which are themselves constituted as immanent unities in the flux of primordial impressions and necessarily constituted one with the other. The appearing thing is constituted because unities of sensation and homogeneous apprehensions are constituted in the primordial flux; therefore, there is always consciousness of something, exhibition [*Darstellung*], more precisely, presentation of something and, in the continuing succession, exhibition of the same. The streams of exhibition [*Darstellungsfluenten*] have such flow and cohesion that what appears in them diverges in multiplicities, formed just so and in just such a way, of shadings of exhibition like the content of sensations in shadings of sensation. Precisely for this reason the multiplicity of apprehension is characterized as presentative, just as immanent impressions are so characterized.

One sees at once that if the primally presented sensible data, outside of primal presentations and the primal retentions and pretentions essentially correlated with them, continuously sustain the apprehensional characters of the spatio-material constitution, then phenomenological time, to which the data of sensation and apprehensions of things pertain, and the spacetime of things must coincide point for point. With every point of phenomenal time that is filled, a point of Objective time also filled manifests itself (by means of the content of sensation and the apprehensions which are found in it).

In view of this, in the vertical lines of the diagram not only

31. Cf. Appendix X: The Objectivation [*Objektivation*] of Time and of the Material in Time, pp. 164ff.

do we have the pervasive vertical coincidence which belongs to the phenomenological constitution of time (according to which the primal datum E_2 and the retentional modification O' and E_1' are united in a moment), but also the retentional shadings (which belong to each vertical line) of the apprehensions of things as such stand in pervasive coincidence. There are two coincidences, therefore. The line of apprehensions of things coincides, not only so far as it co-constitutes a continu-

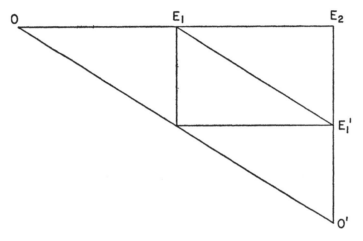

ous succession but also so far as it constitutes the same thing. The former is a coincidence of connecting essential similarity, the latter a coincidence of identity, because in the continuous identifying of the succession we are conscious of what endures as identical. Naturally, also pertaining to this is the continuous, successive identifying of vertical line with vertical line by the fulfillment of protentions which now also have Objective-spatial sense.

The analogy between the constitution of immanent and transcendent unities has already been indicated. As "shadings of sensation" [*Empfindungs-Abschattungen*] (primal data of exhibition for unities of sensation in phenomenological time) have their law, their essential character, in the primal succession, and, through the modification reproduced in the diagram, they constitute the unity of sensation, so do matters also stand with shadings of things or with "appearances," which now function as primal data of the primal succession. The primal succession of moments of appearance, by virtue of the time-founding retentions, and the like, constitutes appearance (altered or unaltered) as phenomenological-temporal unity. In addition, however, appearances from the multiplicity of appearances which belong to the same unaltered thing have an ontic essence (the essence of the appearing thing) which is completely the same—just as the momentary data belonging to an unaltered red are of completely the same essence. Like the lines of alteration of red, the lines of alteration of a thing are also governed by a fixed law. Thus, in one something twofold is intentionally constituted: the appearance and the appearing thing, and in different appearances, either unaltered or altered appearing things.

Now, the question naturally arises: what sort of properties have thing-appearances which are appearances of the same thing? This is the question of the constitution of spatial things, which presupposes, therefore, the constitution of time.

§ 44. Internal and External Perception [32]

Now we shall speak of an enduring perception, i.e., of the perception of things as well as of immanent perception. Along with the perception of things, one also includes under perception continuous perceptual appearance, the continuity of the now-appearance of things, apart from protentional and retentional interweavings. The thing-appearance, the "thing in its orientation," in its determinate exhibition, and so forth, is something that endures just as much as the thing as such which appears. Even a merely apparent surface is something that

32. Cf. Appendix XI: Adequate and Inadequate Perception, pp. 170ff., and Appendix XII: Internal Consciousness and the Comprehension of Lived Experience, pp. 175ff.

endures and in its duration is altered. Properly speaking, I may not speak of "the thing in its orientation" but of the occurrence of the thing-appearance which, if the orientation remains unaltered, continues to endure and otherwise is a continuous flow of alteration of appearances but within a duration.

Even with the perception of an immanent Object, we can take together what is immanent in the now in its continuity; then, however, we have the duration of the Object itself. The Object does not appear in the sense that it does in external perception. Therefore, while in the case of the consciousness of an external Object, "perception" can denote the external appearance of an immanent Object (perception and the perceived being then obviously different), if we speak of internal perception, and at the same time also hold that perception and the perceived are to remain distinct, then the immanent, i.e., the Object itself, cannot be understood under perception. If we speak of internal perception, then we must understand by this either (1) the internal consciousness of the homogeneous immanent Object which is present as constituting the temporal even without a directed glance of attention [*ohne Zuwendung*]; or (2) internal consciousness with the directed glance of attention. In view of this, it is easy to see that the act of directing our attention is the apprehending of an immanent process which has its immanent duration, which coincides with the duration of the immanent sound during the directed glance of attention to it.

In the case of external Objects we have, therefore:

(1) The external appearance.

(2) The constitutive consciousness in which the external appearance as immanent is constituted.

(3) The directed glance of attention, which can just as well be a directed glance of attention toward the appearance and its components as a directed glance of attention toward the appearing thing. Only the latter comes into question when we speak of external perception.

An analogous study must be carried out for memory, the difference being that memory has its own intentionality, namely, that of presentification. Memory has its unity as a process in internal consciousness and has in the unity of immanent time its position and duration. This is true whether the memory is of the immanent or the transcendent. And every remembrance is (if we disregard the directed glance of attention) also remembrance of the immanent. Therefore, while the consciousness of an immanent sound as originary internal consciousness can have no immanent temporality, the presentificational consciousness of an immanent sound (which in an appropriately altered sense is presentificational consciousness of the internal consciousness of the sound) is an immanent Object belonging to immanent temporality.

§ 45. The Constitution of Non-Temporal Transcendencies

We must further observe that every consciousness in a unitary sense (as a constituted immanent unity) is at the same time necessarily also unity of consciousness of the objective to which it "refers." But not every consciousness is itself time-consciousness, i.e., consciousness of something temporal, something constituting intentional time. Thus, a judicative consciousness of a mathematical state of affairs is an impression, but the mathematical state of affairs which in its unity "is there" undivided is nothing temporal; the act of judgment is not an act of presentation (or of presentification).[33] Accordingly, one can say of a thing, an event, or a temporal being that it is represented in phantasy, that it appears according to the mode of phantasy, memory, expectation, or that it appears retentionally: and, likewise, one can say that the thing

33. Cf. Appendix XIII: The Constitution of Spontaneous Unities as Immanent Temporal Objects [Zeitobjekte]—Judgment as a Temporal Form and Absolute Time-Constituting Consciousness, pp. 182ff.

appears as actually present, that it is perceived. But one cannot say that a mathematical state of affairs appears as present or as presentified. The act of judgment can be of long or short duration, has its extensity in subjective time, and can be actually present or presentified. What is judged, however, is not long or short, enduring or less enduring. And so also with regard to what is quasi-judged in the presentification of the judgment. What is presentified is the judgment and not the judged. If one says that he "merely imagines" a state of affairs, this does not mean that the state of affairs is presentified but that it subsists in the character of a modification of neutrality rather than in the character of belief. The modalities of belief in no way coincide with those of the present-not present but cut across them. With regard to an individual state of affairs, one can still speak—unauthentically—of temporal characters so far as the matter which in the state of affairs is logico-analytically articulated and grasped synthetically can be present according to the mode of perception or presentified according to the mode of phantasy. But for a non-temporal state of affairs, i.e., for one that does not in any way deal with the temporal, it makes no sense. To phantasy oneself making a mathematical judgment does not mean to cause the mathematical state of affairs to become an idea of phantasy, as if the state of affairs could be something exhibited which is presenting or presentifying.

Appearance in the pregnant sense of presentation [*Präsentation*] also pertains to the sphere of actual presentation [*Gegenwärtigung*] and its modifications. It pertains to the constitution of the appearing, or, better, to the real givenness of individual being that it is given in the form of a continuity of appearances as exhibitions. That states of affairs can also "merely appear" and demand proof in a real givenness is obvious. This also changes nothing concerning what has been said, namely, that states of affairs ("facts of nature") grounded in individual appearances (natural appearances) attain givenness on the basis of the underlying data of appearance, therefore, in a similar way through infinities of "exhibitions." It spite of this, it must be said that the "exhibition" (appearance) of the state of affairs is not exhibition in the true sense, but rather in a derived sense. The state of affairs is not really something temporal. It subsists for a determinate time but is itself not something in time like a thing or an occurrence. The act of exhibition [*Darstellen*] and the consciousness of time belong not to the state of affairs as such but to the matter of the state.

The same also holds of all other secondary acts and their correlates. A value has no position in time. A temporal Object may be beautiful, pleasant, useful, etc., and may be all this in a determinate time. But the beauty, pleasantness, and so on, have no place in nature and in time. These qualities are not what appears in presentations and presentifications.

ADDENDA AND SUPPLEMENTS TO THE ANALYSIS OF TIME-CONSCIOUSNESS FROM THE YEARS 1905–1910

ADDENDA AND SUPPLEMENTS TO THE ANALYSIS OF TIME-CONSCIOUSNESS FROM THE YEARS 1905–1910

APPENDIX I

PRIMAL IMPRESSION AND ITS CONTINUUM OF MODIFICATIONS [1]

Every primal impression is characterized as such and every modification as such. Further, every modification is a continuous modification. This, indeed, distinguishes this kind of modification from the phantasmal and the figurative. Each of these temporal modifications is a dependent limit in a continuum. And this continuum has the character of a one-sided, limited, orthogonal [*orthoiden*] multiplicity. This multiplicity has its beginning in the primal impression and continues as a modification in a given direction. Pairs of points having like intervals in this continuum constitute temporal phases of Objects, these phases being Objectively the same distance apart.

When we speak of a "modification" we have in mind, above all, the alteration according to which the primal impression

1. To § 12, p. 52.

continuously "dies away." Nonetheless, each modification is obviously to be considered in the same sense as a modification of any given preceding modification. If we abstract any phase of the continuum, we can say that it dies away; and the same is true of any additional phase. This, indeed, is part of the essence of every such (unilaterally directed) continuum. It behaves exactly as in the continuity of intensities spreading out from O. The augmentation is here the modification which every intensity undergoes. Every intensity in itself is what it is and every new intensity is precisely a new one. But in relation to any intensity already given, every phase later in the series can be considered as the result of an operation. If B is the augmentation of A, then C is the augmentation of an augmentation with reference to A. Thanks to the continuity, not every point is simply an augmentation in relation to a preceding one, but an augmentation of an augmentation, and so on *ad infinitum* and infinitesimally—an infinity of modifications, one into the other. Only here there is no beginning point which itself can be considered as an intensity. The beginning is here a null-point. It is part of the essence of every linear continuum that, proceeding from an arbitrary point, we are able to consider that every other point is continually generated from the first, and every continuous generation is a generation through continuous iteration. We can divide every interval *ad infinitum* and with every division we can envision the later points of division produced mediately through the earlier, and thus any given point you choose is finally produced by one of infinitely many augmentations (of which each is the same infinitely small augmentation). It is also thus with regard to temporal modifications—or, rather, whereas with other continua the talk of generation was only figurative, what we have here is a real description. The temporally constitutive continuum is a flux of continuous generation of modifications of modifications. Starting from the actual now, i.e., from the actual primal impression, the modifications in the sense of iterations proceed, but continually forward. They are not only modifications with reference to primal impressions but also, as regards the series, modifications of one another in the order in which they proceed. This is the characteristic of continuous generation. Modifications continuously beget ever new modifications. The primal impression is the absolute beginning of this generation —the primal source, that from which all others are continuously generated. In itself, however, it is not generated; it does not come into existence as that which is generated but through spontaneous generation. It does not grow up (it has no seed): it is primal creation. Does this mean that a fresh now is continuously added on to the now which is modified into a not-now? Or does the now generate, spring up all of a sudden, a source? These are the images. One can only say that consciousness is nothing without an impression. Where something endures, there a goes over into xa', xa' into $yx'a''$, and so on. The generation of consciousness, however, goes only from a to a', from xa' to $x'a''$. On the other hand, the a, x, y is nothing generated by consciousness; it is the primally generated, the "new," that which comes into existence foreign to consciousness, that which is received as opposed to that which is generated through the spontaneity proper to consciousness. The unique quality of the spontaneity of consciousness, however, is that it merely brings about the growth, the development of the primally generated. It creates nothing "new." Of course, what empirically we call becoming or generation refers to Objectivity, and this is something else again. Here it is a matter of the spontaneity of consciousness, or more circumspectly, the primal spontaneity of consciousness.

Now, the moment of origin—according as it is a matter of the primal source of the now of the constituted content or of the spontaneous generations of consciousness in which the identity of this now continues into the past—is either primal impression or primal remembrance, primal phantasy, etc. If we follow the order of succession of the strata, then every

131

moment of origin of a stratum is the primal source of spontaneous generations which go through the additional strata in their continuous transformations and which represent this moment of origin therein (the moment, that is, which belongs simply and solely to the stratum which is first apprehended). Further, every moment of origin is a phase of a continuous series of such moments which go over into one another through a succession of strata. In other words, every moment of origin helps to constitute a concrete duration, and it belongs to the constitution of a concrete duration that an actual now corresponds to every point of this duration; on its side, this now requires for its constitution a proper moment of origin. These moments in the succession are continuously one, "go continuously over into one another." The transition is "qualitatively" established and, at the same time, is also temporal. The quasi-temporal character is a constant one.

PRESENTIFICATION AND PHANTASY—IMPRESSION
AND IMAGINATION [1]

"Presentification" in the broadest sense and "phantasy" in
the broadest sense, i.e., in the sense of general, although not
completely unambiguous, discourse, are not the same thing.
In the first place, we have non-intuitive memories and other
presentifications, and these we would never call phantasies.
On the other hand, we certainly say, in the case of an intuitive
presentification, that what is remembered hovers before us "in
phantasy" (or at least we can say something like this). However, we do not call the memory itself a phantasy. Presentification, moreover, can be a self-presentification or a symbol-
izing (analogical) one. In the last case, we should say that
what is presentified hovers before us "in the form of a phantasy-image" or is symbolized in a phantasy-appearance. Then
the phantasy-image is the business of phantasy, but that which
goes beyond it, the reference to what is portrayed, is no longer
such. One cannot characterize what is portrayed itself as appearing in the phantasy, as if here two phantasies, one constituted on top of the other, lay before him. Wherever phantasy is mentioned, i.e., phantasy of an object, it is at all times
common to say that the object appears in an appearance—
specifically, in a presentifying appearance—not in a presentative one. What is implied by this? What is meant here by

1. To § 17, pp. 63ff.

133

"appearance"? An object can be intuited; it can be represented "symbolically" (through signs); finally, it can be represented as empty. The intuition (likewise, the empty representation) is a simple, immediate idea of the object. A symbolic idea is a secondary idea, mediated by a simple one, and is empty. An intuitive idea brings about the appearance of the object, an empty one does not. To begin with, then, we can divide simple ideas into those which are empty and those which are intuitive. An empty idea can, however, also be a symbolic one which not only represents the object voidly but also represents it "by means of" signs or images. In the last case, the object is symbolized, made intuitive in an image, but is not "itself" intuitively represented. Every intuitive presentation of something objective represents it according to the mode of phantasy. It "includes" a *phantasy-appearance* of the objective. At the same time, the presentification can have the character of *actuality* or *inactuality* [2] and the mode of certainty (that of the point of view) can be anything whatsoever: certainty, conjecture, supposition, doubt, etc. Further, it is a matter of indifference whether the presentification apprehends the objective thing as past or as existing now (though, with expectation, if it visualizes what is expected, then we already have a symbolic consciousness). The "mere phantasy-appearance" remains at all times as the common nucleus. The problem here, of course, is to explain how this nucleus is clothed, so to speak, with all the rest, how the apprehension of the nucleus is connected with further apprehensions. So also we find an appearance with all simple presentations; for example, we find an appearance underlying symbolic visualizing presentations—not now a phantasy-appearance but a perceptual one. Therefore, we distinguish perceptual appearances and phantasy-appearances; the latter include material of apprehension, "phantasms" (presentifi-

2. "Actuality" and "inactuality" here have the same meaning as "potentiality" and "neutrality" in the sense of the *Ideen*.

cational modifications of sensations), the former, sensations.

In what way, then, is a phantasy-appearance a modification (a presentifying modification) of the corresponding perceptual appearance? Naturally not from the side of the modes of the modalities of the point of view, which have nothing to do with the matter at all. On the other hand, we have a modification irrespective of the possible changes of these modes. To sensations correspond the phantasms; however, the apprehensions (and the complete appearances) are also reciprocally modified; in fact, they are modified in the same respect, the apprehensions irrespective of their modality. If it is also true that the apprehension and the complete appearance require a qualitative mode, then this still has nothing to do with that "imaginative" modification of which we speak here.

Independently of the mode of the "point of view," we call a perceptual appearance [*Erscheinung*] an Appearance [*Apparenz*],[3] or, more clearly, a *perceptive* [perzeptive] Appearance when it occurs in a perception (mode of belief), and an *illusory* Appearance when it occurs in an illusion. On the other hand, we must also distinguish between an *impressional* Appearance (Appearance of sensation) and an imaginative Appearance, which in turn can be the content of a memory, of an illusion in memory, and the like. The Appearance, therefore, as the identical nucleus of all intuitive acts, concerns the difference between impression and imagination, and this difference conditions the difference between presentation and presentification for the whole phenomenon. It is further evident that this difference between impression and imagination concerns not only the sphere of "external sense" but also that of internal. In other words, all the modal characters with which the Appearance can be connected, and the correlative ontic characters (the character "real" as existing, as having existed, as coming to be, i.e., as coming to occur [*eintreten*],

3. As with the pair *Objekt-Gegenstand,* to differentiate the terms *Erscheinung* and *Apparenz* I have translated *Erscheinung* by *appearance* and *Apparenz* by *Appearance*. J.S.C.

the character of illusion, of presentificational being-now, etc.), serve as a basis for the split into impression and imagination— so also with wishing, willing, and so on. At the same time, however, in the sphere of "internal sense" we must distinguish between sensation and Appearance just as we did in the sphere of external sense. In the case of Appearance, however, we must distinguish between the Appearance itself and its modal characters. Thus, for example, I believe this or that. This belief is actual belief, is an impression. To this belief corresponds a phantasm "belief." This belief in itself, or the sensation of belief, is to be distinguished from the act of belief in apprehension as my state, my act of judgment. I have perceptual consciousness of myself and my act of judgment, and in this apprehension we must distinguish the internal Appearance and the modality of the act of belief, which posits being (my act of belief) and enters into existing reality. It is enough to separate the "act of belief" and the "apprehension" of this act without taking this apprehension as psychological apperception, which posits the immanent in connection with the real world.

Therefore, every consciousness has the character either of "sensation" or of "phantasm." Every consciousness, every "sensation" in the broadest sense, is precisely something "perceptible" and "imaginable" or something rememberable, i.e., in every way capable of being experienced. Ever and again, however, we have consciousness which has its possible counterpart in phantasm.

THE CORRELATIONAL INTENTIONS OF PERCEPTION
AND MEMORY—THE MODES OF TIME-
CONSCIOUSNESS [1]

Let us now consider the mode of consciousness "remembrance." As unmodified consciousness, it is "sensation" or
what amounts to the same thing, impression. Or, more clearly,
it may include phantasms, but it itself is not the modification
according to phantasy of another consciousness as the corresponding sensation. However, an Appearance is included
therein. I remember something past; in the remembrance is
contained the imaginary Appearance of the occurrence, which
appears with a background of Appearance to which I myself
belong. This total appearance has the character of an imaginative Appearance, but in a mode of belief which characterizes
memory. We can then posit the memory itself in the phantasy,
can have memory in the phantasy and also in the memory. I
dwell on [lebe in] a memory and the memory suddenly emerges
"that I have remembered such and such," or I phantasy that I
have a memory. At the same time, to be sure, we find the
modality of the memory transformed into a corresponding
phantasm, but the matter of the memory, the memory-Appear-
ance, is not itself further modified any more than the phantasms contained in it have been further modified. There is no
phantasm of the second level. And the entire memory-Appear-

1. To § 33, pp. 96ff.

ance making up the matter of the memory is phantasm and likewise does not undergo further modification.

If, furthermore, I then have a memory of memory, there appears in association with a process of remembrance—i.e., a consciousness in which imaginary Appearances in the qualitative mode of remembrance stand forth and run off—a "modified" remembrance. In view of this, essentially the same is to be said as before. The qualitative mode of the simple memory is replaced by "memory of memory," i.e., I have a phantasm of memory (going along with that of the entire process of remembrance). But the phantasm of memory is a character of memory of . . . based on an imaginary Appearance, and this is identically the same in the case of simple memory and memory-of-memory [*Erinnerungs-Erinnerung*]. If one says that it is characteristic of memory, in contrast to everything that forms its content, that there is an apprehension which supplies the reference of the memory to the actual perceptual reality, this is certainly correct but changes nothing of what has been said. With regard to this apprehension itself, then, we must distinguish the content and the mode of belief. In the case of simple memory, which, let us say, I now have, the apprehension is naturally a different one from that of the memory-of-memory, in which the remembered memory refers to a remembered now as the point of actuality. But the principal thing here is that the Appearances (which we take wholly empirically, just as appearances) can undergo no modification. And the same is true for the contents of the apprehensions of memory, which give the Appearances reference to the now, these naturally being not completely intuitive.

This reference to the actual now, which is the characteristic of memory and distinguishes it from "mere phantasy," is not, however, to be grasped as something added on externally. This reference has an obvious analogue in the reference of every perception to an actual here. Furthermore, just as every memory points to an infinite nexus of memory (to something

138

earlier), so every perception points back to an infinite nexus of perception (a manifold infinity). (The here is not perceptible thereby, i.e., not itself given in the memory.) We can now also take a perception purely for itself, outside its nexus. However, this nexus, although not really present as the connection of the perception with additional perceptions, nevertheless lies "potentially" in the intention. That is, if we consider the complete perception at any moment, it still has connections, in the sense that belonging to it is a complex of determinate or indeterminate intentions which leads further and which when evaluated is fulfilled in additional perceptions. This nexus of intentions is not to be cut away. As far as the individual sensation is concerned, it is in truth nothing individual. That is, the primary contents are at all times bearers of rays of apprehension [*Auffasungsstrahlen*] and never occur without these rays, no matter how indeterminate the latter may be. The same thing is true of memory. It has in itself its "nexus," i.e., as memory it has its form, which we describe as forward-and-backward-directed intentional moments, without which it cannot be. Its fulfillment requires lines of memories which discharge into the actual now. It is impossible to separate the "memory for itself" without regard to the intentions which connect it with others. It is equally impossible to detach these intentions themselves.

"Memory for itself" already has these intentions. There is no "mere phantasy" to be gathered from it. But one might say that memory is still memory of a former now, a quasi-perception, which brings about consciousness of a temporal flow. Why shouldn't we hold fast to the entire phenomenon and be able to cut away the real intentions of memory on either side? This question may be answered as follows: the perception itself, the "originary" act, not only has its nexus of spatiality but also its nexuses of temporality. Every perception has its retentional and protentional halo. The modification of a perception must also—in a modified way—contain this double halo, and what distinguishes "mere phantasy" from memory is that this whole intentional complex has at one time the character of actuality, at another that of inactuality.

Every sensation has its intentions, which lead from the now to a new now, and so on: the intention toward the future and on the other side the intention toward the past. As far as memory is concerned, it also has its memorial intentions of the future. These intentions are fully determinate insofar as their fulfillment (provided they, in general, are at our disposal) proceeds in a definite direction and is fully determined with regard to content. However, in the case of perception the intentions of the future are in general not determined with regard to their matter and are first determined through the actual additional perception. (What is determined is only that after all something will come.)

As regards the intentions of the past, they are wholly determinate but reversed, so to speak. There is a definite connection between the actual perception and the chain of memories, but it is such that the intentions of memory (as unilaterally directed) terminate in the perception. Now these memories are obviously only possibilities; they are only exceptionally, or only a few of them, actually given with the perception. On the other hand, it is still true that the perception is endowed with matching intentions of the past, but with empty ones, corresponding to those memories of nexuses of memories. Not only the empty just-past, which has its orientation on the actual now, but also, as one might well say, vague, empty intentions which concern what lies further back are directed toward the now. These intentions become actualized or attain fulfillment in that, so to speak, through recollection we go back at a bound to the past and then again intuitively presentify the past progressively to the now. One can say that the present is always born out of the past, naturally, a determinate present out of a determinate past. Or better, a determinate flux ever and again runs its course. The actual now sinks away and goes over into a fresh now, and so on. If this is a necessity of an *a priori* kind, still it implies an "association," i.e., the past nexus is determined experientially, and further determined is "that something or other will come." But we are now led from this secondary factor (the complex of temporal intentions of experience) to the originary one, and this subsists in nothing other than in precisely the transition from the actual now to the new now.

Now it pertains to the essence of perception that it not only has a punctual now in view and has dismissed from view a just-having-been (and yet, in the characteristic manner of the "just-having-been," is "still conscious of") but also that it goes over from now to now and fore-seeing [*vorblickend*] faces each one. The wakeful [*wache*] consciousness, the wakeful life, is a living-in-face-of [*Entgegenleben*], a living from one now toward the next. By this, we are not merely or primarily thinking about attentiveness. Rather, it seems to me that independently of attentiveness (in the narrower and in the broader sense) an originary intention goes from now to now, being linked with the now indeterminate, now more or less determinate intentions of experience which spring from the past. These, indeed, trace out the lines of linkage. The regard from the now to the new now, this transition, however, is something originary, which first smooths the way for future intentions of experience. I said above that this belongs to the essence of perception; it is better to say that it belongs to the essence of impression. It is certainly true of every "primary content," of every sensation. "Phantasm" and content of memory imply the corresponding modification of this consciousness, as "as-if consciousness" [*Gleichsam-Bewusstsein*]. And if it is to be real memory, an ordering into the past belongs to this as-if consciousness. The modification of consciousness consists in this, that the entire originary consciousness of the moments concerned preserves its modification fully and completely. This is also true, therefore, of the temporal intentions in whose nexus the impressional regard wholly and completely belongs, and it is in general true of the entire intentional nexus in which that originary impression fits and from which it receives its character.

We consider sensation as the primordial time-consciousness. In it is constituted the immanent unity color or sound, the immanent unity wish or favor, and so on. The activity of phantasy is the modification of this time-consciousness; it is presentification. In it are constituted presentified color, wish, and so on. However, presentification can be memory, expectation, or also "mere phantasy," in which case we cannot speak of *a* modification. Sensation is presentative time-consciousness. Presentification is also sensation, is actually present, is constituted as unity in presentative time-consciousness. The differences between now-presentation and just-now-presentation [*Soeben-Gegenwärtigung*], which together belong to concrete presentation-consciousness, come into question only as modes of presentative time-consciousness. Furthermore, this is also true of the difference between actual presentation, which in itself has its now-presentation phase, and independent autonomous retention, which indeed has reference to the actual now but itself does not include a now-presentation, e.g., the consciousness of a tone which has just sounded. Accordingly, we have as essential modes of time-consciousness: (1) "sensation" as actual presentation and essentially entwined with it but also capable of autonomy, retention, and protention (originary spheres in the broader sense); (2) positing presentification (memory), co-presentification, and re-presentification (expectation); (3) phantasy-presentification as pure phantasy, in which all the same modes occur in phantasy-consciousness.

RECOLLECTION AND THE CONSTITUTION OF TEM-
PORAL OBJECTS [*Zeitobjekten*] AND OBJECTIVE
[*objektiver*] TIME [1]

I can "repeat" the perception of a temporal Object, but in
the succession of these perceptions is constituted the consciousness of two like temporal Objects. Only in recollection
can I have repeated an identical temporal object. I can also
verify in recollection that what is perceived is the same as
that which is subsequently recollected. This takes place in
the simple remembrance, "I have perceived that," and in the
recollection of the second level, "I have a memory of that."
Thus the temporal Object can become a repeated experiential
act. If the Object has been given once, then it can be given as
often as you like, examined again and in different acts, which
then form a succession, can be identified.

Recollection is not only re-consciousness [*Wiederbewusst-
sein*] on behalf of the Object, but as the perception of a
temporal Object it carries its temporal horizon with it, so
that recollection also repeats the consciousness of this horizon.
Two recollections can be memories of like Objects, e.g., two
like sounds. However, they are recollections of the same temporal Object not when the mere content of duration is the
same but when the temporal horizon is the same, when, therefore, both recollections fully and completely repeat one an-

1. To § 32, pp. 94ff.

other with regard to intentional content, apart from differences in clarity or obscurity, incompleteness, etc. The identity of temporal Objects, therefore, is a constitutive product of unity of certain possible coincidences of identification of recollections. Temporal Objectivity is established in the subjective temporal flux, and to be identifiable in recollections and hence to be the subject of identical predicates is an essential part of this Objectivity.

Actually present time is oriented, is ever in flux and always oriented from a new now on. In recollection, time is indeed also given as oriented in every moment of the memory. But every point exhibits an Objective temporal point which can be identified again and again, and the interval of time is formed from purely Objective points and is itself identifiable again and again. What is the identical Object here? The series of primal impressions and continuous modifications, a series of similarities which establish self-coincident forms of lines of likeness or difference but within a general likeness—this series provides primordial consciousness of unity. In such a series of modifications we are necessarily conscious of a unity, the enduring sound (constantly like or altered), and from another point of view, the duration, in which the sound is one, and changes or does not change. And the sound continues; its duration "becomes greater," and the sound "ceases," is over. Its entire duration has expired and moves more and more into the past. Therefore, it, the sound, is given here, let us say, as a sound perpetually unchanged in its duration. But this sound unchanged in its duration—with regard to content—undergoes an alteration which concerns not the content but the entire mode of givenness of the "content in its duration." If we adhere to the phenomenon, we quite certainly have different forms of unity. There is constant change of the modes of givenness, but through the lines of change which conform to every point of the duration, there is a unity: the tonal point. But apart from this identity, the tonal point is ever and again something other, namely, in the mode of temporal depth [*Zeittiefe*]. On the other hand, the continuity of the temporal flux provides unity, that of the flux of a changing or unchanging content, of the temporal object. It is this unity which moves into the past. With it, however, we still do not have complete temporal Objectivity.

The possibility of identification belongs to the constituting of time. I can again and again carry out a reminiscence (recollection), can always produce "again" any portion of time with its filling, and then in the succession of re-productions which I now have, can comprehend the same—the same duration with the same content, the same Object. The Object is a unity of consciousness which in repeated acts (therefore, in temporal succession) can appear as the same; it is that which is identical with regard to intention, which is identifiable in no matter how many acts of consciousness, that is, perceptible or re-perceptible in as many perceptions as you like. I can satisfy myself "at any time" of the identical "it is." Thus an occurrence in time, for example: I can experience it for the first time; I can experience it again in repeated re-experiences and grasp its identity. I can come back to it again and again in my thinking and can verify this thinking through originary re-experience. Thus Objective time is first constituted and, to begin with, that of the just-past, with reference to which the process of experience in which duration is established and every retention of the entire duration are mere "shadings." I have a primordial schema, a flux with its content, but in addition a primordial multiplicity of "I can": I can go back to any place in the flux and produce it "once more." As with the constitution of Objective spatiality, we also have an optimum here. The image of the duration in a simple retrospective glance [*Rückblick*] is unclear. In clear re-production [*Wiedererzeugungen*] I have it "itself," and more clearly, the more nearly complete.

THE SIMULTANEITY OF PERCEPTION AND
THE PERCEIVED [1]

With what right can we say that the act of perception and
the perceived are simultaneous? For Objective time—from
the naïve standpoint—this is not correct, for it is possible
that in the temporal point of the perception the perceived
Object no longer exists at all (e.g., a star). From this standpoint, one must indeed say that the temporal point of the
perception and of the perceived always diverge.

Let us now consider—from the standpoint of phenomenology—appearing Objective time in which a transcendent
Object endures. Then, the duration of the perception does
not coincide with the duration of the perceived Object. We
say that the Object was already in existence before the perception and will continue to exist after the perception has
expired. One can say, however, that the Object is the correlate
of a possible continuous perception which follows it up from
the beginning to the end of its duration. Then, a perceptual
phase corresponds to every phase of the duration of the
Object. We do not assert by this, however, that the beginning
point of the duration of the Object and that of the perception
must coincide, and that, accordingly, the temporal points of
phases corresponding to one another must be identical. Instead of this, we must take into account that the data of

1. To § 33, pp. 96ff.

146

sensation which play their role in the constitution of a transcendent Object are themselves constituted unities in a temporal flow. With the moment in which apprehension begins, perception also begins; prior to this one cannot speak of perception. The apprehension is the "animation" [*Beseelung*] of the datum of sensation. We must still ask, however, whether it begins conjointly with the datum or whether the latter—even if only during a time-differential—must be constituted before the animating apprehension can begin. It appears that this last idea is correct. For in the moment in which the apprehension begins, a part of the datum of sensation has already expired and is only retentionally retained. The apprehension, then, animates not only the momentary phase of primal sensation but also the total datum, including the interval which has expired. This means, however, that the apprehension posits the Object in the state corresponding to the running-off of sensation for the whole duration of this running-off—also, therefore, for the segment of time which precedes it, i.e., the perceptual apprehension. Accordingly, there is a temporal difference between the beginning point of the perception and the beginning point of the Object. Through the clarification of the "external conditions" which govern the emergence of a datum of sensation, the above-mentioned naturalistic contention concerning the non-simultaneity of the perception and the perceived may also perhaps be made intelligible.

Let us now exclude the transcendent Object and ask ourselves how things stand in the immanent sphere as regards the simultaneity of the perception and the perceived. If we understand perception here as the act of reflection in which immanent unities attain givenness, then this act presupposes that something is already constituted—and retentionally preserved—on which it can look back. On this view, therefore, the perception follows the perceived and is not simultaneous with it. But, as we have seen, reflection and retention presuppose the impressional "internal consciousness" of the immanent datum concerned in its primordial constitution, and this datum is concretely one with the actual primal impressions and inseparable from them.[2] If we also denote "internal consciousness" as "perception," then we have here in fact strict simultaneity of the perception and the perceived.

2. Concerning "internal consciousness" cf. Appendix XII, pp. 175ff.

APPENDIX VI

COMPREHENSION OF THE ABSOLUTE FLUX—PER-
CEPTION IN THE FOURFOLD SENSE [1]

The Objects in question here are temporal Objects which
must be constituted. The sensible nucleus (the appearance
without apprehension) is "now" and has just been and has
been still earlier, and so on. In this now there is also retention of the past now of all levels of the duration of which we
are now conscious. Every past now retentionally harbors in
itself all earlier levels. A bird just now flies through the sunlit
garden. In the phase which I have just seized, I find the retentional consciousness of the past shadings of the duration
likewise in every fresh now. But the time-train [Zeitschwanz]
is itself something which sinks back in time and has its own
shading. The entire content of every now sinks into the past;
this sinking, however, is no process which is reproduced ad
infinitum. The bird changes its place; it flies. In every situation, the echo of earlier appearances clings to it (i.e., to its
appearance). Every phase of this echo, however, fades while
the bird flies farther on. Thus, a series of "reverberations"
pertains to every subsequent phase, and we do not have a
simple series of successive phases (let us say, every actual
now with a phase) but a series with every individual successive phase.

Following the phenomenological reduction, every temporal

1. To § 34, p. 98.

149

appearance, therefore, is reduced to such a flux. The consciousness in which all this is reduced, I cannot myself again perceive, however. For this new perceived entity would again be something temporal which referred back to a constitutive consciousness of just such a kind, and so on, *ad infinitum*. The question arises, therefore, whence can I have knowledge of the constitutive flux? [2]

The levels of the description (and of the constitution) of temporal Objects are the following, according to the explanations given hitherto. We have:

1. The properties of empirical Objects in the usual sense: there they are, etc.

2. In the phenomenological view, I take the Object as a phenomenon. I am directed toward the perception, toward the appearance and the appearing in their correlation. The real thing is in real space, endures, changes in real time, and so on. The appearing thing of perception has a space of appearance and a time of appearance. And, in turn, the appearances themselves and all forms of consciousness have their time, namely, their now and their temporal extensity in the form of now-previously [*Jetzt-Vorher*]: subjective time.

Yet we must take into consideration that the Object of perception appears in "subjective time," the Object of memory in a remembered time, the Object of phantasy in a phantasied, subjective time, the expected Object in an expected time. Perception, memory, expectation, phantasy, judgment, feeling, will—in short, everything which is an Object of reflection appears in the same subjective time, i.e., in the same time in which Objects of perception appear.

3. Subjective time is constituted in absolute, timeless consciousness, which is not an Object. Let us reflect now as to how this absolute consciousness attains givenness. We have a tonal appearance; we pay attention to the appearance as such. In such a thing as the sound of a violin (materially considered)

2. Cf. § 40, pp. 110ff.

the tonal appearance has its duration, and in this duration its constancy or alteration. I can pay attention to any phase of this appearance whatsoever (appearance is here the immanent tonal stimulus, apart from its "significance"). This, however, is not the final consciousness. This immanent sound is "constituted," i.e., continuous with the actual tonal now; we also have tonal shadings. In fact, exhibiting itself in these is the interval of tonal pasts which belong to this now. We can in some degree attend to this series. With a melody, for example, we can arrest a moment, as it were, and discover therein shadings of memory of the past notes. It is obvious that the same holds true for every individual note. We have, then, the immanent tonal now and the immanent tonal pasts in their series or continuity. In addition, however, we must have the following continuity: perception of the now and memory of the past; and this entire continuity must itself be a now. In fact, in the living consciousness of an object, I look back into the past from the now-point out. On the other hand, I can grasp the entire consciousness of an object as a now and say: Now I seize the moment and grasp the entire consciousness as an all-together, as an all-at-once. I hear just now a long whistle. It is like an extended line. At any moment, I stop and the line is extended from there on. The regard from this moment embraces an entire line and the consciousness of the line is grasped as simultaneous with the now-point of the whistle. Therefore, I have perception in a multiple sense.[3]

1. I have a perception of the steam whistle, or rather of the whistle of the steam whistle.

2. I have a perception of the content of the sound itself which endures, and of the tonal process in its duration, apart from its disposition in nature.

3. I have a perception of the tonal now and at the same time attend to the conjoined just-having-been of the sound.

4. I have a perception of time-consciousness in the now. I

3. Cf. § 17, pp. 63ff., and § 18, pp. 64ff.

attend to the now-appearing of the whistle, in other words, of a sound, and to the now-appearing of a whistle extending in such and such a way into the past (a now-whistle-phase and a continuity of shading appears to me in this now).

What difficulties are there with regard to the last of these perceptions? Naturally, I have time-consciousness without this itself being again an Object. If I make an Object of it, it itself again has a temporal position, and if I follow it from moment to moment, it has a temporal extensity. There is no doubt that such perception exists. As an apprehending regard can attend to the flux of tonal phases, so it also can attend to the continuity of these phases in the now of their appearing, in which the material-Objective [*Dinglich-Objektive*] is exhibited, and again to the continuity of alteration of this momentary continuity. And the time of this "alteration" is the same as the time of the Objective. If it is a question, for example, of an unaltered sound, then the subjective temporal duration of the immanent sound is identical with the temporal extension of the continuity of the alteration of the appearance.

But do we not have something most highly remarkable here? Can we in a real sense speak here of an alteration where a constancy, an unaltered, filled-out duration is not even thinkable? No possible constancy can be compared to the continuous flux of the phases of appearance.

There is no duration in the primordial flux.[4] For duration is the form of an enduring something, an enduring being, something identical in the temporal series which last functions as its duration. With occurrences such as a storm, the motion of a meteorite, etc., it is a question of uniform nexuses of alteration of enduring Objects. Objective [*Objektive*] time is a form of "persistent" objects, their alterations, and other processes concerned with them. "Process" is, therefore, a concept which presupposes persistence. Persistence, however, is a unity which is constituted in the flux, and it pertains to the essence of flux that there can be nothing persistent in it.

4. To the following, compare in particular § 36, p. 100.

In the flux there are phases of lived experience and continuous series of phases. But such a phase is nothing persistent and just as little is it a continuous series. Certainly, it is also in a way an objectivity. I can direct my regard toward a prominent phase in the flux or toward a part of the flux and identify it in repeated presentification, come back to it again and again and say: *this* part of the flux. And so also for the entire flux, which I can identify in a specific way as this one. But this identity is not the unity of something which persists, and never can be such. It pertains to the essence of persistence that what persists can persist either altered or unaltered. Ideally, every alteration can pass over into constancy, motion into rest and conversely, qualitative alteration into constancy. The duration is then filled with the "same" phases.

In principle, however, no part of what is not-flux can appear. The flux is not a contingent flux as an Objective one is. The variation of its phases can never cease and pass over into a self-continuing of ever-like phases. But in a certain sense is there not also something abiding about the flux, even though no part of the flux can change into a not-flux? What is abiding, above all, is the formal structure of the flux, the form of the flux. That is, the flowing is not just flowing in general; rather, each phase is of one and the same form. The stable form is always newly filled with "content;" however, this content is not something brought into the form from the outside but is determined by the form of regularity [*Gesetzmässigkeit*]—but in such a way that this regularity does not alone determine the concrete. The form consists in this, that a now is constituted through an impression and that to the impression is joined a train of retentions and a horizon of protentions. This abiding form, however, supports the consciousness of a continuous change (this consciousness being a primal matter of fact, namely, the consciousness of the transformation of the impression into retention), while an impression is continuously present anew or, with reference to the quiddity of the impression, the consciousness of the change

153

of this quiddity while the latter, which until just now we were still cognizant of as "now," is modified into the character of "just-having-been."

With this interpretation we come, therefore—as we have already intimated earlier—to the question of the time-consciousness in which the time of the time-consciousness of tonal appearances is constituted.

If I live in the appearing of the sound, the sound stands forth to me and has its duration or alteration. If I attend to the appearing of the sound, then this appearing stands forth and now has its temporal extension, its duration or alteration. In view of this, the appearing of the sound can signify different things. It can, in addition, signify attending to the continuities of shading: now, just-now, and so forth. Now the stream (the absolute flux) must again be objective and have its time. Also, there would again be necessary a consciousness constituting this Objectivity and one constituting this time. In principle, we could again reflect upon this, and so on *ad infinitum.* Is the infinite regress here to be shown as innocuous?

1. The sound endures, is constituted in a continuity of phases.

2. While or as long as the sound endures, to every point of the duration there belongs a series of shadings from the now on into the blurred past. We have, therefore, a continuous consciousness, of which every point is a stable continuum. This continuum, however, is again a temporal series to which we can attend. Thus the business begins afresh. If we fix any point of this series, it appears that a consciousness of the past must pertain to it, which consciousness refers to the series [*Serie*] of past series [*Reihen*], and so on.

Even if reflection is not carried out *ad infinitum* and if, in general, no reflection is necessary, still that which makes this reflection possible and, in principle (or so it seems, at least) possible *ad infinitum* must be given. And here lies the problem.

THE CONSTITUTION OF SIMULTANEITY [1]

A, a sound, let us say, is constituted in a temporal point of a determinate phase of its duration by means of a primal impression α, to which it and the modification, together with the primal generation of new impressions (new now-moments), are joined. Let B be a simultaneous immanent unity, a color, let us say, and let us fix our eyes on it in a point "simultaneous" with the tonal point in question. To this in the constitution corresponds the primal impression β. Now what do α and β have in common? What does it mean to say that they constitute simultaneity and that the two modifications α' and β' constitute a having-been-simultaneous?

Various primal impressions, primal phantasies, etc.—in short, various moments of origin (we can also say: primal moments of internal consciousness)—can belong to a single stratum of internal consciousness. All primal moments belonging to a stratum have the same character of consciousness, which is essentially constitutive for the "now" concerned. It is the same for all constituted content; the mutuality of the characters constitutes simultaneousness, "like-now-ness" [Gleich-Jetzigkeit]. In virtue of the primordial spontaneity of internal consciousness, every primal moment is a source-point for a continuity of generations, and this continuity is of one and the same form. The mode of generation, the primally

1. To § 38, pp. 102ff.

temporal modification, is the same for all primal moments. This regularity can be described as follows: the continuous generation of internal consciousness has the form of a one-dimensional, orthogonal multiplicity; all primal moments within a stratum undergo the same modifications (they generate the same moments of the past). Therefore, modifications of two primal moments which belong to the same stratum (modifications which have the same interval from the corresponding primal moments) belong to one and the same stratum. Furthermore, modifications which belong to a stratum always generate from themselves only modifications which belong to the same stratum. The generation always proceeds at the same rate.

Within every stratum the different points of the continuous series have a different interval from the primal moment. This interval of any given point is identical with the interval which the same point has from its primal moment in the earlier stratum. The constituting primal field of time-consciousness is a continuous extension which consists of a primal moment and a determinate series of iterated modifications, i.e., iterated with regard not to content but to form. The determinations of these modifications are, as regards form, everywhere the same in all primal fields (in their succession). Every primal moment is precisely a primal moment (now-consciousness), every past is a consciousness of the past, and the degree of pastness is something determinate. To it corresponds a fixed, determinate, formal character in primally constitutive consciousness.

In the succession of strata, moments of like "content," i.e., of like internal states, can occur again and again as primal moments. These primal moments of different strata which have an internal content that is completely similar are individually distinct.

APPENDIX VIII

THE DOUBLE INTENTIONALITY OF THE STREAM OF
CONSCIOUSNESS [1]

In the stream of consciousness we have a double intentionality. Either we consider the content of the flux with its
flux-form—we consider then the series of primal lived experience, which is a series of intentional lived experiences,
consciousness of . . . ; or we direct our regard to intentional
unities, to that of which we are intentionally conscious as
homogeneous in the streaming of the flux. In this case there
is present to us an Objectivity in Objective time, the authentic
temporal field as opposed to the temporal field of the stream
of lived experience.

The stream of lived experience with its phases and intervals
is itself a unity which is identifiable through reminiscence
[Rückerinnerung] with a line of sight [Blickrichtung] on what
is flowing: impressions and retentions, sudden appearance and
regular transformation, and disappearance or obscuration.
This unity is originarily constituted through the fact of the
flux itself; that is, its true essence is not only to be, in general,
but to be a unity of lived experience and to be given in internal
consciousness, in which a shaft of attention [aufmerkender
Strahl] can go to the flux (the shaft itself is not attended to;
it does not enrich the stream, nor does it alter the stream
which is to be taken notice of but "fixes" and makes objec-

1. To § 39, pp. 105ff.

157

tive). The attentive perception of this unity is an intentional lived experience with variable content, and it can direct memory to what is gone by and repeat it as modified, compare it with its like, and so on. That this identifying is possible, that here an Object is constituted, lies in the structure of lived experience, namely, that every phase of the stream changes into retention "of," this again, and so on. Without this, no content would be thinkable as lived experience. Lived experience would not otherwise necessarily be given to the subject as unity and could not be so given; consequently, it would be nothing. The flowing consists in a transition of every phase of the primordial field (therefore, of a linear continuum) through a retentional modification of the same, only just past. And so it continues.

With the second intentionality, I do not pursue the flux of the field, nor that of the form "now (original)-retentional modification of different levels" as a homogeneous series of transformations; rather, I direct my attention toward what is intended in every field and in every phase which the field has as a linear continuum. Every phase is an intentional lived experience. With the preceding objectivation [*Vergegenständlichung*] the constitutive lived experiences were the acts of internal consciousness whose objects are precisely the "phenomena" of temporally constitutive consciousness. These are themselves, therefore, intentional lived experiences. Their object is the temporal points and temporal durations with their actual, objective fullness. While the absolute temporal flux flows, the intentional phases are displaced, but so that in a correlative way they constitute unities, pass over into one another just like phenomena of the one [*von Einem*], which shades off in flowing phenomena so that we have "objects in a modal setting" and in an ever new modal setting. The form of the modal setting is the orientation: the actually present, the just past, the futural. With reference to objects, we can again speak of the flux in which the now is changed into what is past, etc. And this is necessarily predelineated *a priori* through the structure of the flux of lived experience as a flux of intentional lived experience.

Retention is a characteristic modification of perceptual consciousness, which is primal impression in the primordial, temporally constitutive consciousness, and, with reference to temporal Objects, whether or not it is consciousness of the immanent—as an enduring sound in the tonal field or a color-datum in the visual field—, perceptual consciousness is immanent (adequate) perception. If $P(s)$ is the perception of a sensed sound which apprehends the latter as an enduring sound, then $P(s)$ changes into a continuity of retentions $R_P(_s)$. $P(s)$, however, is also given in internal consciousness as lived experience. If $P(s)$ changes into $R_P(_s)$, then the internal consciousness of $R_P(_s)$ also necessarily changes in internal consciousness. For here, indeed, being and inwardly-being-conscious-of [*Innerlich-bewusst-sein*] coincide. Now the internal consciousness of $P(s)$ also changes into the retentional modification of this internal consciousness, and we are inwardly conscious of this modification. Therefore, we are aware of the just-having perceived.

If a perception of a sound goes over into its corresponding retention (the consciousness of the sound which has just been) a consciousness of the act of perception which has just been is present (in internal consciousness as lived experience) and both coincide. I cannot have one without the other. In other words, both necessarily belong together, the passing of the object-perception to a retentional modification of this perception and the passing of the act of perception to a retentional modification of this act. We necessarily have, therefore, retentional modifications of two kinds given with every perception which is not a perception of internal consciousness. Internal consciousness is a flux. If in this flux lived experiences which are not "internal perceptions" are to be possible, there must be retentional series of two kinds. Thus with the constitution

159

of the flux as unity through "internal" retention there must in addition be a series of "external" ones. The latter series constitutes Objective time (a constituted immanence, external with regard to the former but still immanent). At the same time, we must note that internal consciousness does not have, as a correlate, immanent data which endure (such as a tonal datum, or enduring joys, sorrows, or those enduring processes called judgments), but the phases constituting these unities.

Appendix IX

PRIMAL CONSCIOUSNESS AND THE POSSIBILITY OF REFLECTION [1]

Retention is not a modification in which impressional data really remain preserved, only in an altered form. Rather, retention is an intentionality, in fact, an intentionality of a special kind. When a primal datum, a new phase, emerges, the preceding one is not lost but is "retained in concept" (i.e., "retained" exactly), and thanks to this retention a looking back to what has expired is possible. Retention itself is not an act of looking back which makes an Object of the phase which has expired. Because I have the phase which has expired in hand, I live through [*durchlebe*] the one actually present, take it—thanks to retention—"in addition to" and am directed to what is coming (in a protention).

But because I have this phase in hand, I can turn my regard toward it in a new act which—depending on whether the living experience which has expired is being generated in a new primal datum (therefore, is an impression), or whether, already completed, it moves as a whole "into the past"—we call a reflection (immanent perception) or recollection. These acts stand to retention in the relation of fulfillment. Retention itself is not an "act" (i.e., an immanent unity of duration constituted in a series of retentional phases) but a momentary consciousness of the phase which has expired and, at

1. To § 39, especially pp. 105ff., and § 40, pp. 110ff.

the same time, a foundation for the retentional consciousness of the next phase. Since each phase is retentionally cognizant of the preceding one, it encloses in itself, in a chain of mediate intentions, the entire series of retentions which have expired. The unities of duration which are reproduced through the vertical lines of the diagram of time and which are the Objects of the retrospective acts are constituted precisely in this way. In these acts the series of constitutive phases together with the constituted unity (e.g., the enduring sound, retentionally preserved unaltered) attains givenness. It is thanks to retention, therefore, that consciousness can be made an Object.

We can now raise the question: What about the beginning phase of a self-constitutive lived experience? Does it also attain givenness only on the basis of retention and should we be "unconscious" of it if no retention followed thereon? On this it can be said that the beginning phase can become an Object only after its running-off in the way indicated, through retention and reflection (or reproduction). But were we aware of it only through retention, what its designation as "now" bestowed on it would be incomprehensible. The beginning phase could at most only be negatively distinguished from its modifications as that phase which does not make us retentionally conscious of any preceding ones. But consciously it is, of course, positively characterized throughout. It is certainly an absurdity to speak of a content of which we are "unconscious," one of which we are conscious only later. Consciousness is necessarily *consciousness* in each of its phases. Just as the retentional phase was conscious of the preceding one without making it an object, so also are we conscious of the primal datum—namely, in the specific form of the "now"—without its being objective. It is precisely this consciousness that goes over into a retentional modification, which then is retention of this consciousness itself and the datum we are cognizant of originally in it, since both are inseparably one. Were this consciousness not present, no retention would be thinkable, since retention of a content of which we are not conscious is impossible. As for the rest, primal consciousness is nothing inferred by reason but can be beheld in reflection on the constituted living experience as the constituting phase exactly as in the case of retention. One may by no means misinterpret this primal consciousness, this primal apprehension, or whatever he wishes to call it, as an apprehending act. Apart from the fact that it would be an obviously false description of the state of affairs, one would also in this way get involved in insoluble difficulties. If one says that every content attains consciousness only through an act of apprehension directed thereon, then the question immediately arises as to the consciousness in which we are aware of this act, which itself is still a content. Thus the infinite regress is unavoidable. However, if every "content" necessarily and in itself is "unconscious" then the question of an additional dator consciousness becomes senseless.

Furthermore, every act of apprehension is itself a constituted unity of duration. During the time that it is built up, that which it is to make into an Object is long since gone by and would be—if we did not already presuppose the entire play of primal consciousness and retentions—no longer accessible to the act at all. However, because primal consciousness and retentions are on hand, the possibility exists. in reflection of looking to the constituted lived experience *and* the constituting phases, and even becoming aware of the differences which exist, for example, between the primordial flux as we are conscious of it in primal consciousness and its retentional modifications. All the objections which have been raised against the method of reflection can be explained as arising from ignorance of the essential constitution of consciousness.

APPENDIX X

THE OBJECTIVATION [*Objektivation*] OF TIME AND
OF THE MATERIAL IN TIME [1]

Parallel problems are the constitution of the one all-space
[*All-Raumes*] which is co-perceived with every particular perception so far as the perceived thing as regards its substance
appears lying in it, and the constitution of the one time in
which lies the temporality of the thing, in which the duration
of the thing is ordered, as well as the duration of the things
and material processes which pertain to the environment of
the thing. In this same time the ego is also ordered, not only
the physical self [*Ichlieb*] but also its "psychical lived experiences." The time pertaining to every material thing is its time
and yet we have only one time—not only in the sense that
things are ordered beside one another in a unique linear extension but also that different things or processes appear as
simultaneous. They do not merely have parallel similar times
but one time, numerically one. The situation is not the same
here as with a manifold of spatial fullness where visual and
tactile fullness coincide. Rather, here we have separated, non-
coincident materialities which endure and are still in the
identical temporal interval.

Material givenness takes place as a process in phenomenological temporality. The total flow of motivating sensations
of motion (K) and the "images" (i) motivated by means of

1. To § 43, pp. 117ff.

164

them are temporally extended. In the transition from K_o to K_1, the images motivated in this way have their discharge i_o—i_1 and stand in temporal coincidence with K. As is the case with every temporal flux that is fulfilled, this one also has its temporal form, and this form can be a changing one. The flow of K and therewith that of i can follow quickly or more slowly, and yet in the most diverse ways, at a like or unlike speed according as the temporal fullness spreads out in the temporal interval, fills this or that partial interval with greater or lesser "thickness" [*Dichte*]. Further, the running-off of K and therewith the succession of images can be reversed, and again in a changing temporal form. The temporal forms of the consciousness of a givenness conform to this.

In certain respects, all this is irrelevant to the Object which appears and stands forth as given. This is also the case with the greater or lesser extension of the kinesthetic image-discharge or the greater or lesser discharge of possible appearances from the ideal total multiplicity. I say irrelevant so far as indeed at all times the same thing, static and unaltered as to content, let us say, is there, ever spreading out its material fullness of content in the same temporal form and in uniform thickness throughout. And yet the temporality of the flux has something to say for the Objectivation. It appears, indeed, that something temporal, temporality itself, belongs essentially to the appearing object and, in our case, temporality in the form of the duration of the unaltered, static thing. But one may now say that the Objectivation of time must still have its "exhibitive" content in the phenomenon, and wherein otherwise than in its phenomenological temporality? More precisely, the appearance in the narrower sense of the term, that falling under the actual motivating circumstances, will naturally come into question, and as in this appearance, the image exhibits the Objectively local through its localness [*Ortlichkeit*], through its quasi-shape and quasi-size, its Ob-

165

jective shape and size, and, further, through its quasi-coloration, the Objective coloration, so through its temporality it exhibits Objective temporality. The image is the image in the flux of the continuity of images. To every image-phase in this flux corresponds the appearing Objective temporal phase of the thing, more precisely, the side of the Object which exhibits itself in this image. The pre-empirical temporal position of the image is the exhibition of the Objective position; the pre-empirical temporal extension in the running-off of the continuity of images is the exhibition of the Objective temporal extensity of the thing, therefore, its duration. All this is self-evident.

Observed more closely, this "exhibition" of Objective time is, to be sure, one essentially other than that of the thing existing in Objective time, enduring in it as identical in time, and filling time in the mode of duration. If, for the sake of simplicity, we assume a continuity of like images (therefore, of like richness) within the limited sphere of "clearest seeing," then an intentional bundle of rays goes through the images flowing off in quasi-time so that by this means the images are posited in unequivocal correspondence. Points lying on the same intentional ray exhibit through their contents one and the same Object-point. Here, therefore, a unity-positing consciousness goes through the pre-empirical temporal continuity. A flux of content, strung along the intentional ray, exhibits phase for phase the same material point [Dingpunkt]. Every image-point also has its pre-empirical temporal position. However, a consciousness of unity does not again go through the successive temporal positions, Objectifying them to identical unity. The point-series of images spreading out in this countinuity of temporal positions exhibits the same thing-point [Ding-Punkt]; however, the series of temporal positions does not exhibit an identical temporal point of the same thing-point but again a temporal series. And the individual image-point has the same temporal position as all other co-existing image-points. The entire image has a temporal position, and every different image a different position. Every different temporal position in the pre-empirical flux of images exhibits a different Objective temporal position. Otherwise, indeed, a thing which as such has its duration, a filled, Objective temporal series, would not appear.

The consciousness of unity, spreading out in the pre-empirical flow of time, posits unity in the temporal flow of the exhibitive images, in that it turns every image into precisely an exhibitive one, posits givenness in it and with every new image, givenness "of the same." What is given in every phase, however, is given and posited as a now with such and such a content. In the transition to the next phase it is held fast in its now. Thus the new phase (and every new phase) is given with its now held fast; therefore, in the continuous transition, the phases are so posited in unity that every phase in the Objectivation keeps its now, and the series of now-points (as Objective temporal points) is filled with a continuously uniform and identical content. When phase a is actual, it has the character of the actual now. But in the temporal flux, phase joins to phase, and as soon as we have the new actual phase those which have just "now" been have altered their character as actual. In this flux of alterations, temporal Objectivation takes place so far as, in the flux of phenomenological alteration which a undergoes in sinking back, a continuous positing of the identical a with the determinate temporal point results. In Objectifying consciousness, the flux of images running off appears as a flux of alterations of sensible contents. If every image with its now were so Objectified as it is in itself, the unity of this multiplicity would be the unity "lying in it," and to be inferred from it.

In the Objectivation of a thing, however, the image-content, in the sense of the kinesthetic unity of motivation, is thus and thus apprehended. It is not, therefore, simply accepted as it is but as exhibition, as the bearer of an intentional

167

bundle characterized as thus and thus and always being fulfilled in the mode of pure coincidence. This intentionality
pervades the image-content, while every now-moment which
belongs to the actual image undergoes the same temporal
point-Objectivation which it would even without the Objectivation of the thing. An Objective temporal series, therefore,
is everywhere constituted in the same way. However, the
series of appearances in whose flux Objective temporality is
constituted is, with respect to its matter, different according
as it is material or non-material temporality which is constituted, e.g., according as Objective time is constituted in the
duration of alteration of an immanent sound or of a thing.
Both series of appearance have something in common, a
common form which makes up the character of the Objectivation of time as such. However, the appearances are at one
time appearances of the immanent, at another of the material.
Thus comes to be the identity of the sound in the flux of
tonal phases, each of which has its temporal individuation and
a unity in the continuity of phases, comprising an identity of
sound which exists in all phases and consequently endures.
Thus the identity of the thing in the flux of appearances is
identity of the thing appearing in all appearances in the mode
of self-and-now-givenness, the thing which appears in an ever
fresh now and consequently endures.

At the same time, it must be stressed that in transcendent
perception the phases of the earlier appearance do not merely
remain retentionally preserved, as occurs with every sequence
of appearances or at least occurs within certain limits. The
actual perceptual appearance at any given time does not
conclude with what it brings to actual givenness, the reality
posited by the perception as now. It is not true that the
preceding appearances are merely preserved as appearances
of what have been. The (primary) consciousness of memory
of earlier phases is memorial consciousness, to be sure, but
with regard to the earlier perception. What was perceived

168

earlier not only is present now as the earlier perceived but is taken over into the now and is posited as still in being now. Not only is what is just really perceived posited as now but also what has been given previously. During the flux of real perception not only is what is really seen posited as enduring being in the flux of its appearances but also what has been seen. And the same is true with regard to the future. Posited as now in the expectation of additional phases of real perception is also the about-to-be-perceived. The about-to-be-perceived is now; it endures and fills the same time. Precisely the same thing holds for everything unseen but capable of being seen, i.e., everything which could be perceived with the possible flowing-off of K as belonging to it.

There is accomplished here only an extension of the Objectivation of time which we have discussed under the limitation of what is continually seen and what in the course of the seeing again and again exhibits itself differently. Everything seen can also be unseen but still remains capable of being seen. In conformity with its essence, every flux of perception admits of an extension which finally transforms the perceived into a not-perceived. However, just as the positing of time, since it identifies the visual thing which appears there "complete" in the succession of its complete appearances, co-objectifies every temporal position of the phases of the appearance and gives it the significance of an Objective temporal position, with the result that an Objective enduring thing is displayed in the series of appearances, so also takes place and in a similar way the positing of time with regard to the totality of appearances. These appearances bring about the exhibition of one and the same Objectivity in a way which is always incomplete.

ADEQUATE AND INADEQUATE PERCEPTION [1]

Adequate perception as pure, immanent, and adequate givenness of an object can be grasped in two senses, one of which is closely analogous to external perception, while the other is not. In the immanent hearing of a sound I can take a double line of apprehension: one with regard to what is sensed in the temporal flux, the other with regard to what is being constituted in this flux and yet is still immanent.

1. The sound may fluctuate as regards quality or intensity or may be present to me as enduring in a completely unaltered internal determinateness. In any case, I encounter a flux, and only in this flux can such an individual Objectivity be given to me. The sound begins as a tonal now and there continually follows thereon an ever new now, and every now has its content, on which I can direct my regard as it is. Thus I can swim in the stream of the flux, follow it up with my intuitive regard. Moreover, I can also pay attention not to the momentary content alone but to the whole extension, which here means the flux together with its concrete fullness, or in abstraction from the latter. This flux is not the flux of Objective time, which I determine with watch and chronometer, not world-time, which I fix in relation to the sun and the earth, for this is capable of phenomenological reduction. Rather, we call this flux pre-empirical or pre-phenomenological time.

1. To § 44, pp. 122ff.

It offers the primordial representatives for the representation of Objective-temporal predicates, speaking analogically: temporal sensations. With the described perception, we attend to the actual temporal content in its temporal extension and in the given mode of its fulfillment of this extension, or we attend to the temporal content *in abstracto* or to the temporal extension *in abstracto*—in any case to the really given, to what is really inherent as a moment of perception.

2. On the other hand, however, if the sound, let us say, the tone C endures, our perceptive intention can be directed to the tone C which there endures, i.e., to the object, tone C, which in the temporal flux is one and the same object, ever the same in all phases of the flux. And again, if the tone varies, let us say, on the side of intensity or even as regards its quality, fluctuating, for example, this way of speaking already indicates a line of perception which has something identical in view that changes or remains the same while its quality and intensity vary. What is identical is, therefore, another object than heretofore. There it was the temporal flux of the sounding of the tone; here it is the identical in the flux of time.

The temporal flux of the sounding of the tone is time: time that is filled out and concrete. However, this flux itself has no time, is not in time. But the tone is in time, it endures, it changes. As that which is identical in change, it is "substantially" one. But as the time is pre-empirical, phenomenological time, so the substance of which we are speaking here is pre-empirical, phenomenological substance. This substance is the identical, the "bearer" of the changing or the persisting, for example, of the persisting quality and the changing intensity, or the continuously changing quality and the abruptly altering intensity, etc. In talking of "substance," our regard is directed toward the identical as opposed to the temporal content, which changes from phase to phase and which now is like, now different. It is something identical which unites all temporal phases of the flux through the unity of the common

171

essence, therefore, of what is generically common, which last, however, is not generally brought out in an essential abstraction and taken for itself. The identical in the flux is the self-maintaining, continuous, common essence in its individuation. In viewing substance, we do not practice abstraction from the flux of the content given in the act of viewing and direct our regard to the general. Rather, the flux of temporal fullness is kept in view and from the flux the identical that is in it and remains bound to it is beheld.

Substance is the identical in the full, concrete flux. If by abstraction we throw into relief a dependent element such as, for example, the intensity of a sound, there is also to be found here an act of identification of the same kind, for we say that the intensity persists or is altered. These identities are phenomenological accidents. The sound, the phenomenological "thing," has different "properties" and each of these is again something identical in its persistence and alteration. This identical element is, so to speak, a dependent ray of substantial unity, an aspect of substance, a dependent moment of its unity but in itself, and in the same sense, something unitary. Substance and accident in this pre-empirical sense are phenomenological data. They are data in possible perceptions, i.e., adequate perceptions. These perceptions are, as I said, related to external perceptions. In fact, external perceptions are likewise perceptions of things or accidents of things, and the character of these perceptions is analogous to the character of the perceptions of immanent phenomenological substance.[2] When we perceive a house, this object has its temporal extensity, and this belongs to the essence (therefore, to the essence of the signification of perception). It appears as enduring unaltered, as the identical in this duration, as persisting in temporal extensity. If we take something in external perception which is changing, a bird in flight or a flame

2. Substance naturally is not understood here as real substance, the bearer of real properties, but merely as the identical substrate of the phantom-perception.

whose light intensity varies, the same thing holds true. The external thing has its phenomenal time and appears as the identical element of this time, namely, as the identical as regards motion and alteration. To be sure, however, all these perceptions are inadequate; time with its fullness is not adequately given, is not exhibitable as sensation. And, likewise, the identity of the thing and its properties is not to be adequately realized, not for example, like the identity of the sound in its sounding, in the flux of its dying away and swelling again, and so on. It is evident, however, that basically the same identification or substantialization which in immanence is adequately given or effected is present in external perception as inadequate, being effected on the basis of transcendent apperception. It is also clear that every analysis of the signification of a thing or property first goes back to the immanent-phenomenological sphere, and here it must bring to light the essence of phenomenological substance and accident—just as every clarification of the essence of time leads back to pre-empirical time.

We have, accordingly, learned to recognize significant types of adequate and inadequate perception. With reference to the terms "internal" and "external" perception, it is now evident that they provoke certain doubts. That is, according to the above it is to be noted that the term "internal perception" is ambiguous. It means something essentially different on both sides, namely, at one time perception of an immanent component of perception, at another perception of something immanent which is seen but not the perception of a part. If we compare both types of adequate perception, we find it common to them that adequate givenness of their objects is achieved and all unauthenticity [*Uneigentlichkeit*], all transcendent interpretation is excluded. But only in the one mode of perception is the objective a real constituent of the phenomenon of perception. The temporal flux of the sounding is there with all its components in the phenomenon of perception, and makes it up. Every phase, every component of this flux is a part of the phenomenon. On the other hand, what is identical in the temporal flux, the phenomenological substance and its properties, that which persists or varies, is indeed something adequately to be seen in the second mode of perception, but is not to be designated as a real moment or a part of it.

Appendix XII

INTERNAL CONSCIOUSNESS AND THE COMPREHEN-
SION OF LIVED EXPERIENCES [1]

Every act is consciousness of something, but every act is also that of which we are conscious. Every lived experience is "sensed," is immanently "perceived" (internal consciousness) although naturally it is not posited or meant ("to perceive" here does not mean intentionally to be directed toward and to apprehend). Every act can be reproduced; to every "internal" consciousness of the act as an act of perception belongs a possible reproductive consciousness, for example, a possible recollection. To be sure, this seems to lead to an infinite regress; for is not the internal consciousness, the perception of the act (of judgment, of external perception, of rejoicing, etc.) now again an act, and hence itself internally perceived, and so on? On the other hand, we can say: every "lived experience" is in the significant sense internally perceived. But internal perception is, in the same sense, not a "lived experience." It is not itself again internally perceived. Every lived experience which our regard can light upon manifests itself as something enduring, flowing, thus and thus changing. And the intending regard does not create this, but merely looks thereon.

This present, actual, enduring lived experience is, as we can discover through a change in our regard, after all a "unity

1. To § 44, pp. 122ff.

of internal consciousness," of time-consciousness, and this is precisely a consciousness of perception. "Perception" here is nothing other than temporally constitutive consciousness with its phases of flowing retentions and protentions. Behind this act of perception there stands no other such act, as if this flux were itself a unity in a flux. What we call "lived experience," what we call the act of judgment, of enjoyment, of external perception, also the act of observing an act (which is a positing intention)—all these are unities of time-consciousness; therefore they are instances of perceivedness [*Wahrgenommenheiten*]. And to every unity corresponds a modification. More precisely: to the originary time-consciousness, to the perception, corresponds an act of reproduction, and to what is perceived corresponds something presentified.

We now set beside one another, therefore, the originary act and its presentification. The situation is then the following: Let A be any act known in internal consciousness (which has been constituted in it). Then if P_i is the internal consciousness of this act, we have $P_i(A)$. Of A we have a presentification $V_i(A)$; however, this in turn is something of which we are inwardly conscious. Therefore, we have $P_i[V_i(A)]$.

Within internal consciousness and all its "lived experiences" we have, therefore, two kinds of event, A and $V_i(A)$, which correspond to one another.

The whole phenomenology which I had in mind in *Logische Untersuchungen* was that of lived experiences in the sense of data of internal consciousness, and this, at all events, is a closed sphere.

Now A can be something different, for example, a sensible content, let us say, a sensed red. Sensation here is nothing other than the internal consciousness of the content of sensation. The sensation red (as the sensing of red) is therefore P_i (red) and the phantasm of red is V_i (red), which, however, has its own conscious existence $P_i[V_i$ (red)]. Thus it is understood why in *Logische Untersuchungen* I could identify the act of sensation and the content of sensation. If I move within the frame of internal consciousness, there, naturally, we do not find an act of sensation, only what is sensed. It would also be correct, then, to contrast acts (intentional lived experiences of internal consciousness) and non-acts. The latter were precisely the totality of the "primary," of the sensible content. As regards phantasms, on the other hand, it would naturally be wrong (within the frame of internal consciousness) to say of them that they are "lived experiences," for the term *lived experience* signifies givenness of internal consciousness, inward perceivedness. We have, then, to distinguish the presentified content, let us say, the phantasied content of sense, and the presentifications of the same, the $V_i(s)$ and those are intentional lived experiences belonging in the frame of internal consciousness.

Let us now consider the case where A is an "external" perception. It is naturally a unity of internal consciousness. And in internal consciousness there is a presentification of it, as there is of every lived experience. Therefore, $P_e(g)$, like $P_i[P_e(g)]$, has its $V_i[P_e(g)]$. Now it pertains to the essence of perception as such that a parallel presentification corresponds to it, namely, an act which presentifies the same thing that the act of perception perceives. "Reproduction" is the presentification of internal consciousness, which stands in contrast to the originary running-off, to the impression. Presentification of a material occurrence may not then be reproduction. The natural event is not produced once again, it is remembered, it stands before consciousness in the character of the presentified.

Let us now consider the remarkable relationship of both presentifications, obviously different in themselves from one another, which are here to be compared.

1. Over against P_e stands $V_i(P_e)$ or, as we can now also write, $R(P_e)$ (the internal reproduction of external perception).

2. Over against P_e stands V_e (the presentification of the external object e).

Now, there exists an essential law according to which R $(P_e) = V_e$. The presentification of a house, for example, and the reproduction of the perception of this house reveal the same phenomenon.

Furthermore, we can now say that the act of meaning [*Meinen*], which in the specific sense is "Objectifying," can (1) have the character of "internal reflection," of "internal perception" as a positing intention on the basis of that of which we are "inwardly conscious." The act of meaning can accustom itself [*sich hineinleben*] to consciousness, can accept [*nehmen*] internal consciousness as a substrate. Then, as far as possible, all objectivities implicitly on hand in internal consciousness as such attain givenness; they become "objects." In this way, sensations, understood as sensible contents, become objects, and, on the other side, all the acts constituted in internal consciousness as unities, *cogitationes,* the intentional lived experiences of internal consciousness.

(2) In internal consciousness, therefore, we also have "intentional lived experiences," since there we have perceptions, judgments, feelings, cravings, and the like. These unities can function as substrates. Instead of positing them in "internal reflection," i.e., in intentional "internal perception," and objectifying them, an act of meaning enters into their intentionality and thus "takes" away from them the objects implicitly intended in them and makes them intended in the significant sense of the Objectifying act of positing. At the same time, the act which functions as a substrate can be an empty, presentifying one. Naturally, the memory of a joy or a desire, etc., can suddenly emerge and the act of meaning can direct itself toward the agreeable past event, the desired as such, without the vivid idea thereby prevailing.

We must, therefore, distinguish the pre-empirical being of the lived experiences, their being prior to the reflective glance

178

of attention directed toward them, and their being as phenomena. Through the attending directed glance of attention and comprehension, the lived experience acquires a new mode of being. It comes to be differentiated," "thrown into relief," and this act of differentiation is nothing other than the act of comprehension, and the differentiation nothing other than being comprehended, being the object of the directed glance of attention. However, the matter is not to be thought of as if the difference consisted merely in this, that the same lived experience just united with the directed glance of attention is a new lived experience, that of directing-oneself-thither-to; as if, therefore, a mere complication occurs. Certainly when a directed glance of attention occurs, it is evident that we distinguish between the object of the directed glance of attention (the experience A) and the directed glance of attention itself. And certainly we have reason to say that our glance of attention was previously directed toward another, that the directed glance of attention toward A then took place, and that A "was already there" before this act. But we take into consideration that this talk of the same lived experience is very ambiguous and that it is in no way to be inferred directly from this way of speaking (where it finds legitimate application) that phenomenologically nothing has been altered in manner of the modal setting of this "same" for the living experience.

Let us consider the matter more closely. The directed glance of attention, which, as we say, goes at one time this way and at another time that, is also something that is grasped through a new directed glance of attention, and thus becomes primordially objective (in a primordial cognizance of it). Consequently, the setting-in-relation of the object of the directed glance of attention and the directed glance itself and the primordial taking cognizance of this relation constitute also a new phenomenon, just as is the setting-in-relation of the directed glance of attention to the object prior to this act, with the knowledge that this directed glance of attention to the object previously free of it supervenes.

We understand without further ado what it means to have a directed glance of attention toward an object, for example, toward this piece of paper, and, in particular, toward a corner of the paper which is especially prominent. This distinction on the "subjective side," the attending itself in its various steps, is something entirely other than what is specifically noted and not noted in the Object. The object is given in an attentional mode and, if the occasion should arise, we can again direct our attention to the alteration of these modes, precisely to that which we have just described, namely, that, with regard to the object, now this, now that is objective in a particular way, and that what is now specially favored was already there but previously not so favored, that everything favored has a background, an environment in that objective total frame, and so on. It pertains to the essence of this object that it is dependent, that it cannot be without "its" mode of exhibition, i.e., without the ideal possibility of making this an object, and again to pass over from this to the object. It is again part of the essence of the "one and the same" object of which I am conscious in a series that my regard is to be directed toward this very series of modes of exhibition.

These reflections take place in the unity of a time-consciousness. The newly comprehended was—so it is said—already there, belongs to what was previously comprehended as a background, and so on. Every "change of attention" implies a continuity of intentions and, on the other side, in this continuity lies a unity capable of being grasped, a constituted unity, the unity of that which is exhibited only in different attentional changes and from which at any given time different moments or parts are "attended to," "stand in the light."

Now, what is attention other than the running-off of differences of such modes of "consciousness as such," and the

circumstance that such instances of perceivedness go together into one which is in form "the same" and which has
now this, now that attentional mode? What does it mean to
reflect on the moment "directed glance of attention toward"?
At one time, the attentional modes run off "naïvely." In their
running-off, my glance of attention is directed toward the
object appearing in them. At another time, an objectifying
regard is directed toward the series of modes itself. In memory, I can run through the series repeatedly, and as such it
has its unity.

THE CONSTITUTION OF SPONTANEOUS UNITIES AS
IMMANENT TEMPORAL OBJECTS [*Zeitobjekte*]—
JUDGMENT AS A TEMPORAL FORM AND ABSOLUTE
TIME-CONSTITUTING CONSCIOUSNESS [1]

If we have a judgment (e.g., $2 \times 2 = 4$), what is meant as
such is a *non-temporal idea*. The same thing can be meant
in countless acts of judgment in an absolutely identical sense,
and this same thing can be true and false. Let us take this
idea as the "principle" and consider the "judgment" as the
correlate of this principle. Therefore, should one not say, "the
act of judgment, the consciousness in which precisely the
$2 \times 2 = 4$ is meant"? No. Let us consider: instead of directing my glance of attention toward what is meant as such, I
direct it toward the judging, to the process in which it comes
to be given to me that $2 \times 2 = 4$. A process goes on. I begin
with the forming of the subject-thought 2×2 and bring this
formation to an end. This serves as the fundamental affirma-
tion for then affirming "is equal to 4." Therefore, we have a
spontaneous act of forming which begins, goes forward, and
ends. What I form there, however, is not the logical principle
which is meant therewith. What is "formed" is not the meant;
rather, what is formed in spontaneity is first of all the 2×2
and on this, the $2 \times 2 = 4$. As soon as this formation is complete, it is already over as a process, and immediately sinks
back into the past.

1. To § 45, pp. 124ff.

At the same time, what is formed is obviously not the process of formation (otherwise, the comparison in terms of forming would be wrongly employed). I can also attend to the continuously advancing consciousness and to the unity of the advancing process (just as in the perception of a melody I can attend to the continuous consciousness, the continuous running-off of the "phenomena," but not to the notes themselves). But the end of this process is not the completed phenomenon in which precisely $2 \times 2 = 4$ is meant. In just the same way, the process of consciousness constituting the appearance of a hand motion is not the appearance itself in which the hand motion appears. In our case what corresponds to the appearance is the intending that it is true that $2 \times 2 = 4$, the explicit "predication" in which, so to speak, the "it is so" appears. In the unity of the appearances of the hand motion belong not the phases of the processes of consciousness but the phases of appearance being constituted in them. The components of the predication, the subject term, the predicate term, etc., are also constituted in the process of the consciousness of judgment (as the flux of the same). And, after it has been constituted, the subject term of the judgment, as of the unitary intending of the judgment, likewise belongs to the intending of the judgment, although the consciousness of this term is continuously further modified (exactly as the present appearance of the initial phase of a motion, always in the mode of sinking back, belongs to the appearance of the motion; the forms of consciousness, however, in which the initial phase is constituted as the stable phase of the motion, do not so belong).

We must say, therefore, that there are two things to be distinguished:

(1) the flux of consciousness and

(2) what is self-constituting in it,

and from the second side, on the other hand:

(a) the judgment as the self-constituting "appearance" of

183

the intending of $2 \times 2 = 4$, which is a process of becoming, and

(b) that which becomes there, the judgment which stands at the end as the formed, the become: the complete predication.

The judgment is here, therefore, an immanent process of unity in immanent time, a process (not a flux of consciousness but a process which is constituted in the flux of consciousness) which begins and ends and with the end is also over, just as a movement is over in the moment in which it has taken place. Of course, while with the appearance of a sensible perceived becoming it is always conceivable that the becoming may pass over into enduring being or that motion in any given phase may pass over into rest, here rest is, in general, inconceivable.

With the above, however, we have not yet exhausted all distinctions. With every act of spontaneity something new emerges. This act functions, so to speak, in every moment of its flux as a primal sensation which undergoes its shading-off according to the fundamental law of consciousness. The spontaneity which sets about its work in steps in the flux of consciousness constitutes a temporal Object, namely, an Object of becoming, a process, essentially only a process, and not an enduring Object. And this process sinks back into the past. In view of this, one must consider the following: if I begin with a this-positing [*Diessetzung*], then the spontaneous laying hold of and comprehending is a moment which stands forth in immanent time as a moment only to sink away forthwith. To this, however, is joined a retaining [*Festhaltung*] for the formation of the total unity of the process of judgment in immanent time. The primal positing of the this (the "snapping-in" [*Einschnappen*] as Lipps says) passes continually over into the retentive this-consciousness. This retaining is not the preserving of the primal positing, which, to be sure, undergoes its immanent temporal modification, but a form involved with this consciousness. Therewith there is something noteworthy, namely, that in this stable phenomenon is constituted not merely the sinking away of the beginning phase; rather, the continuous self-preserving, self-perpetuating this-consciousness constitutes the this as an enduring posited thing. This implies that beginning and continuing [*Einsetzen und Fortsetzen*] make up a continuity of spontaneity which is essentially grounded in a process of sinking away temporally, which causes the beginning phase and the preserving phase which follow it in the temporal running-off to sink down, and by this also causes to sink down what it brings with itself as supporting ideas (intuitions, empty representations) and modifications of ideas. The act begins, goes on, but in a changed mode as act (as spontaneity), and then a new act, let us say, that of the predicate-positing [*Pradikat-setzung*] begins, continuing this total spontaneous running-off. The result, if the formation does not proceed further, is not the new (in its way) primal-welling spontaneity of the predicate-positing; rather, this positing proceeds from a ground. In the same immanent temporal phase in which the positing occurs, and, indeed, in the form of a retentive spontaneity, in the modified form which it has in contrast to the primal-welling subject-positing, the positing of the subject is really accomplished. On this positing of the subject is built the originary predicate-positing. With this, the subject-positing forms a unity, the unity of the entire judgment as an existing phase of the temporal process, as a temporal moment in which the judgment is actually "completed." This moment sinks away, but I do not immediately cease to judge, i.e., an interval in which the judging is retained is continuously joined, here as otherwise, to the last perfecting moment of accomplishment. By this, the judgment as temporally formed in such and such a way gains a further extension. If the occasion should arise, I again join thereon new, higher formations of judgment, build on them, and so forth.

Consequently, the judgment as an immanent Object in

internal time-consciousness is a unity of a process, a continuous unity of a stable positing (naturally, the positing of a judgment) in which two or more moments of accomplishment, moments of primal positing, appear. This process runs out in an interval without such moments, an interval which in a "neutral" [*zuständlicher*] way is consciousness of this process, belief in that which in a "primordial" way through the moments of accomplishment has attained consciousness. Judgment (predication) is possible only in such a process. This implies, of course, that retention is necessary for the possibility of judgment.

The mode in which a spontaneous unity, e.g., a predicative judgment, is constituted as an immanent temporal Object is sharply distinguished from the mode of the constitution of a sensible process, a continuous succession. The distinction rests on this, that in the latter case the "primordial" element that is the primal source-point of the ever newly filled temporal moment is either a simple primal phase of sensation (its correlate is the primary content in the now) or a similar one formed through an apprehension as a phase of primal appearance. The primordial element in the case of judgment, however, is the spontaneity of positing, which is based on some material or other of affection. The structure, therefore, is, in this respect, already more complex.

Furthermore, a double primordiality appears here. The "primordial" constitutive element for the judgment as a temporal form is the continuity of the "positing," which in this respect is always primordially giving. The continuous moments of judgment of the temporal points, as of the temporal form, are constituted then in time-consciousness with its retentions. But we must distinguish the moments of authentic effective positing of productive spontaneity as opposed to the continuous moments of retentive spontaneity which preserve what is produced. This is a difference in the constituted temporal form in which the source-points are distinguished, and naturally also a difference in the constitutive time-consciousness in which the original phases fell into two modes: the creative and the neutral.

If, accordingly, we may consider the idea of the judgment as of the temporal form in distinction from the absolute, temporally constitutive consciousness as clarified (and precisely therewith the corresponding differences with regard to other spontaneous acts), then we can now say that this judgment is an act of meaning, an analogue of the immanent-Objective appearance in which, for example, an external spatio-temporal being appears. What is meant appears, as it were, in the meaning, in the meaning (of the temporal form) "$2 \times 2 = 4$," precisely the propositional state of affairs, syntactically formed in such and such a way. This state of affairs, however, is no thing, no Objective-temporal being, neither an immanent nor a transcendent one; what is meant in the state of affairs is enduring, but the state of affairs itself is not enduring. Its meaning as meant [*Meinung*] begins; however, it does not itself begin any more than it stops. In conformity with its essence, it can be known or given in various ways. It can be articulated, and then in a determinately constructed spontaneity can be known. This spontaneity as an immanent temporal form can proceed more or less "rapidly." We can, however, also be conscious of the spontaneity in a neutral way, and so on.

Spontaneous temporal forms, like all immanent Objects, have their counter-images in reproductive modifications of themselves. The phantasy of judgment is, like every phantasy, itself a temporal form. The primordial moments of its constitution are the "primordial" phantasies, in contrast to the retentional modifications, which are joined immediately to them according to the basic law of consciousness. Since phantasy is constituted as an immanent Object, the immanent quasi-Object, the unity of what is immanently phantasied, in the immanent quasi-time of phantasy, is also constituted by

187

means of its proper phantasy-intentionality, which has the character of a neutralized presentification. And where the phantasy is a presentifying modification of an "appearance," there is also constituted the unity of a transcendently phantasied thing, let us say, the unity of a phantasied spatio-temporal Object or the unity of a phantasied state of affairs, one that is quasi-given in a quasi-judgment of perception or quasi-thought in a phantasy-judging of another kind.

Printed and bound by CPI Group (UK) Ltd, Croydon, CR0 4YY

09/06/2025

14685936-0001